Invitation to History

Starter:

From the Middle Ages
to the Age of Absolutism

Cornelsen

Materialien für den bilingualen Unterricht: Geschichte
Invitation to History
Starter: From the Middle Ages to the Age of Absolutism

Erarbeitet von:
Annegret Weeke, Düsseldorf

Didaktische Mitwirkung:
Dieter Langhammer, Oberndorf

Redaktion:
Ingrid-Maria Sauer (verantwortliche Redakteurin), Christine Finke, Mailin Neubauer (Assistenz), Friederike Terpitz, Ralph Williams

Bild- und Textrechte:
Dr. Ilka Soennecken

Illustration:
Hannes Geipel, Berlin

Umschlaggestaltung:
Klein & Halm Grafikdesign, Berlin

Layout und technische Umsetzung:
zweiband.media, Berlin

Invitation to History: Starter – Handreichungen für den Unterricht auf CD-ROM (ISBN 978-3-06-033240-3) enthält vertiefende Aufgabenblätter zu den im Schülerbuch behandelten Themen und Kompetenzen.

www.cornelsen.de

1. Auflage, 2. Druck 2015

Alle Drucke dieser Auflage sind inhaltlich unverändert
und können im Unterricht nebeneinander verwendet werden.

Druck: Firmengruppe APPL, aprinta Druck, Wemding

ISBN 978-3-06-033026-3

Preface

Invitation to History: Starter is the first volume of your bilingual history book. Six units cover the period from the Middle Ages to the 17th century. In each unit you will find the following elements:

Texts

The texts give you an overview of the subject. Words with an ▶ arrow are important history terms, places or people and are explained in the Glossary of terms and persons or in the list of the UNESCO World Heritage sites (see Appendix, pp. 86-91). **Key terms** in the text are printed in bold and are listed on the unit revision page.

Sources

Sources (**S**) for your work are: texts, cartoons, portraits, statistics, photographs, maps and paintings. They are numbered throughout in each unit.

History skills

History skills introduce you to the work of historians. They give you the language and tools for analysing the different kinds of sources.

Key terms

These boxes give you further information on key terms.

New vocabulary

All numbered words[1] are explained or translated on the same page.

Tasks

In each section you'll find different kinds of tasks which will help you to understand an event or development.

Activate your English

These boxes will help you to write and speak about historical topics.

Unit revision

At the end of the units there are activities to revise key events, terms and personalities, as well as practice using history skills and vocabulary.

Appendix

The Appendix gives you a Glossary of terms and persons, a Glossary of historically important places (UNESCO World Heritage sites), an English-German vocabulary list in alphabetical order, and a list of useful vocabulary to be learned in each unit.

S7 Urban II is giving a sermon at Clermont in 1095, book illumination

Key terms

Native Americans are the group of people who lived in the Americas before the Europeans came. They do not like to be called 'Indians'.

Activate your English

The cartoon is called ...
The cartoon was created by ... in ... (place) in ... (time).

The cartoon shows ... in the centre/on the right/on the left/at the bottom/in the foreground/ background ...

The ... stand(s) for/symbolize(s)/mean(s) ... because ...
The cartoonist shows ... which mean(s) that ...

... (name of cartoon/cartoonist) wants to tell their audience that ...

Contents

Unit 5 Reformation and Conflict

Unit 6 Louis XIV and the Age of Absolutism

Appendix

Unit 1 **Life in the Middle Ages**

1.1 What is left from the Middle Ages?

S[1] 1 ▸ St. Michael's Church *(Michaeliskirche)* at Hildesheim

S 2 The Brunswick Lion *(Braunschweiger Löwe)*

S 3 ▸ Marburg castle *(Marburger Schloss)*

S 4 Reconstruction of a ship which was used by the Hanseatic League

S 5 Throne of the German kings *(Königsthron)* at ▸ Aachen Cathedral *(Aachener Dom)*

S 6 Uta of Naumburg's statue at Naumburg Cathedral *(Naumburger Dom)*

1 S = source *Quelle*

1.2 Germany in the Middle Ages

Around the year 1200 (twelve hundred), most of today's Germany was forest[1]. There were small villages[2] where people had cut down the forest and had their farms. On average[3], these villages had 70 inhabitants[4]. The trips between the villages took a long time and people had to walk through the dark forest.
Only 10 to 20 per cent[5] of all people, or about 800,000, lived in the around 3,000 towns. Today 88 per cent of all Germans live in towns and cities. Only six towns at that time had more than 10,000 inhabitants. The biggest was Cologne (*Köln*) with 40,000.
Altogether there were probably eight million people living in Germany. Today there are 81 million people.

Key terms[8]

Middle Ages
The Middle Ages, or medieval times, is the period[6] of European history from about AD 500 to about 1500 (fifteen hundred).
For historians[7], the Middle Ages began with the end of the ▸ **Roman Empire** (*Römisches Reich*). The beginning of the Middle Ages is often called the "Dark Ages"[9] in English.

Activate your English

Talking and writing about the Middle Ages
The "Middle Ages" and "medieval" are the English terms for "das Mittelalter" and "mittelalterlich". Middle Ages is always spelled with capital letters at the beginning.

The Middle Ages is used with the verb in the singular or plural. So you can say:
The Middle Ages are sometimes called the "Dark Ages" because very few people could read and write.
The Middle Ages were a time of great changes.

The Middle Ages is a period in European history.
The Middle Ages is sometimes divided into early, high and late Middle Ages (Früh-/Hoch-/Spätmittelalter).

Key terms

BC and AD
AD stands for the Latin words *anno Domini*, which means "in the year of the Lord" (*im Jahre des Herrn*). For example, AD 500 means that something happened five hundred years after the birth of Christ.
BC means "before the birth of Christ".[11]

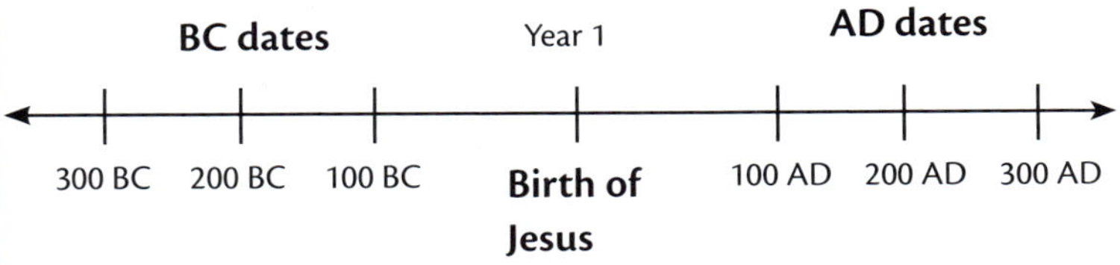

1 forest *Wald*
2 village *Dorf*
3 on average *im Durchschnitt*
4 inhabitant *Einwohner/in*
5 per cent *Prozent*
6 period *(Zeit-)Abschnitt*
7 historian *Historiker/in*
8 key term *Schlüsselbegriff*
9 age *hier: Zeitalter*
10 Latin *Latein*
11 Christ *Jesus Christus*
12 to found *gründen*

Tasks: Germany in the Middle Ages

1 Find out when your hometown or a city nearby was founded[12] and how many people lived there in the Middle Ages.
2 Find out if there are buildings or anything else from the Middle Ages in your area. Take some photos and present them to your class.

1.3 The nobles[1] and their castles[2]

S7 Inside a late medieval stone castle

1 nobles *Adlige*
2 castle *Burg*

Walls
Tapestries[1] were on the walls for decoration.

Great hall
Everyone ate here. The ▸ **lord and lady** sat at the "high table", with their children, guests, and most important knights. They were the first who got their food. Everyone else sat on wooden benches[2]. The tables were taken away after the meals.

Chapel[3]
This was the most important[4] part of any castle. The lord and his family heard morning mass[5] there every day. They had their own priest[6].

Lighting
During the day, light came into the hall through the openings in the walls. They let in wind, snow and rain because in the early Middle Ages there was no glass in the openings.
At night, wooden shutters[7] closed the openings. The only light in the hall came from candles[8].

Heating
A large fireplace[9] heated[10] only one room in the castle. Other rooms were cold in winter.

Entertainment
Travelling jugglers[11], musicians, acrobats and storytellers entertained the people in the castle. The lord and his guests often went hunting[12] just for fun.

Food and drink
Lords and ladies ate more meat than the peasants because they could go hunting. When they had guests, they used expensive spices[13] from India and China. There were no forks, so people used knives and their fingers.

Hygiene
People washed their hands before they began to eat. Servants[14] carried water to the great hall at meal times. People in the castles did not take baths very often because the heating of the water was difficult and expensive.
Toilets were just holes in the walls (latrines). The waste[15] fell down into the moat[16] or river where the water washed it away.

Water
To have enough water was very important in a castle. Normally, there was a well[17], sometimes a hundred meters deep.

Private rooms of the lord and lady
The only heated room in the castle usually was the room of the lady.
The medieval lady was responsible[18] for:
- the castle's kitchen and meals
- entertaining guests
- the castle, when her husband was not there.

Rooms for the servants

1 tapestry *Wandteppich*
2 bench *Bank*
3 chapel *Kapelle*
4 important *wichtig*
5 mass *Messe, Gottesdienst*
6 priest *Priester, Pfarrer*
7 shutter *Fensterladen*
8 candle *Kerze*
9 fireplace *Kamin*
10 to heat *heizen, erhitzen*
11 juggler *Jongleur*
12 to go hunting *auf die Jagd gehen*
13 spice *Gewürz*
14 servant *Diener/in*
15 waste *Abfall, Abwasser*
16 moat *Burggraben*
17 well *Brunnen*
18 to be responsible for sth. *für etw. verantwortlich sein*

1.4 From wooden castles to stone castles

S8 Modern drawing of an early medieval wooden castle (a "motte")

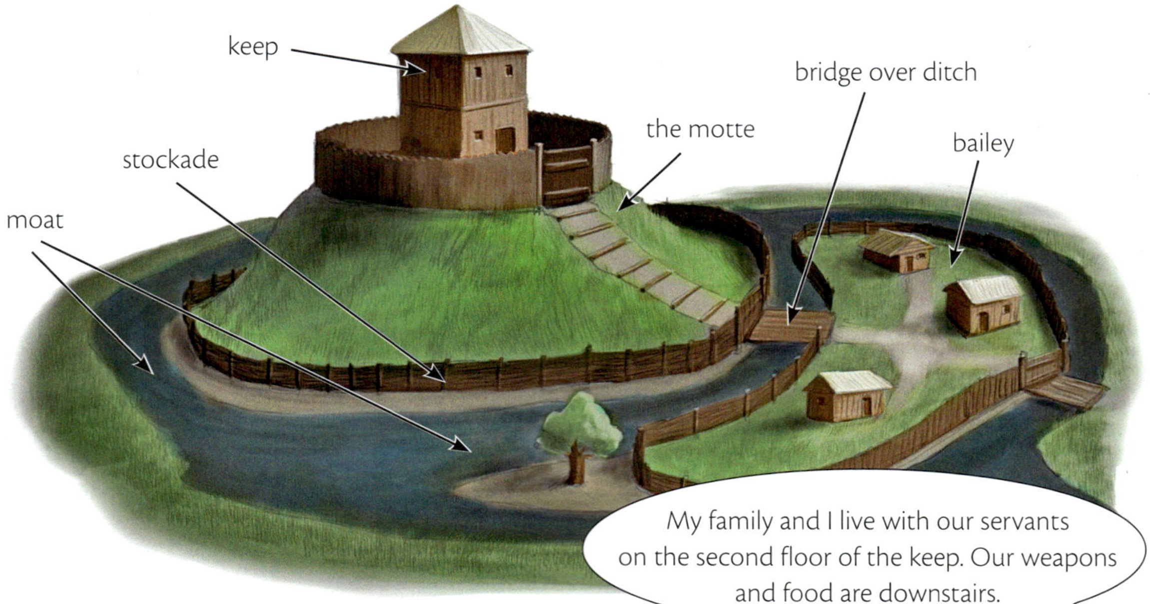

Noble lords[1] lived in castles in the 12th century, but they were mostly not the stone castles which we visit today. The early castles were wooden towers which were called "keeps". They were built on a natural hill or upon stone and earth (= motte). The bailey[2] in front of it was large enough to hold and protect[3] the animals of the lord and his peasants[4]. The moat[5] around the motte was muddy so the attackers[6] sank in it. The grass on the hill made it slippery to climb. From the top, people shot[7] arrows and threw stones at attackers.

S9 Late medieval stone castle

1 noble lord *Adelsherr*
2 bailey *Burghof*
3 to protect sb./sth. *jdn./etw. beschützen*
4 peasant *Bauer/Bäuerin*
5 moat *Burggraben*
6 attacker *Angreifer/in*
7 to shoot arrows *Pfeile schießen*

Task: Safe inside the castle

1 Describe how castles changed between the Early Middle Ages and the Late Middle Ages.

Safe behind thick walls?

S 10 **A trebuchet[1] (ca. 1130)**

S 11 **A cat[2] (ca. 1325)**

S 12 **Crossbowmen[3] (15th century)**

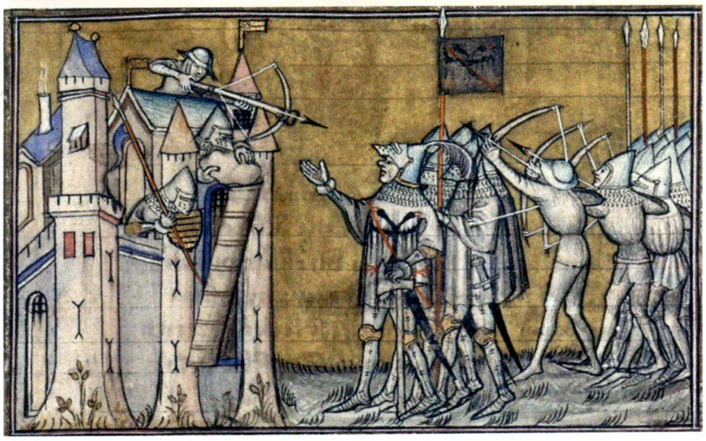

S 13 **A scaling ladder[4] (ca. 1470)**

Tasks: Are the people inside the castle safe?

1 Match the letters of the sentences to the correct number of the pictures. Some pictures go with more than one sentence.
  a They threw large stones at the same parts of the walls for days until the walls fell down.
  b Attackers used them to climb to the top of the castle walls. This was always dangerous because the defenders would try to push them away.
  c Attackers pushed them to the castle walls on wheels. They lowered a drawbridge[5] onto the tower so that the attackers could get onto the walls. Others stood away from the walls because it was a better place from which to shoot arrows into the castle.
  d Attackers moved it to the walls of the castle to hack away at the walls. The wooden roof was kept wet with water to protect the men against fire.
  e They were perfect for shooting through the openings in castle walls.

2 Explain to the class what attackers could do to get inside the castle.

1 trebuchet *Blide/ Wurfschleuder*
2 cat *"Katze", mobiles Belagerungsgerät*
3 crossbowman *Bogen-schütze*
4 scaling ladder *Sturmleiter*
5 drawbridge *Zugbrücke*

Noble lords are professional warriors[1]

The beginning of the Middle Ages was a dangerous time in Europe.
The Vikings (*Wikinger*) from Scandinavia (*Skandinavien*) attacked towns and castles in England, France and Western Germany in the 9th century[2]. The Hungarians (*Ungarn*), who were coming from the East of Europe, attacked[3] Germany.
Noble lords fought[4] against each other for new land all the time. They had a group of warriors on horses with them who fought for them. These warriors were called **knights**[5].
Their horses and armour were very expensive. A war horse, for example, cost the same as four oxen. The armour and the weapons[6] cost another eighteen oxen. Because of these costs, a peasant could never become a knight.

The warriors' pay[7]

In theory[8], all the land in a country was the ▸ **king's or the emperor's**[9] land, but he gave most of it to the noble lords. To get land, they and their knights had to come and fight when the king needed them. The noble lords then did the same: they gave parts of their land to the knights who fought with them. So the warriors' pay was not money but land, with peasants who worked it.

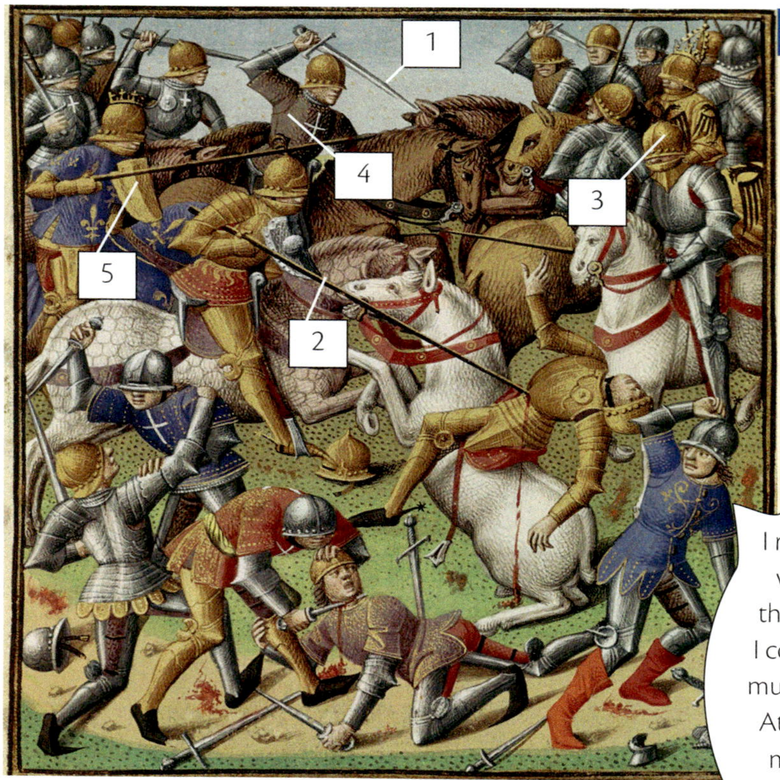

S 14 Knights in battle[10], 15th. century

1 sword[11]
2 lance[12]
3 helmet[13]
4 chaincoat[14]
5 shield[15]

I remember it well: I was seven when my father took me to the Duke of Brunswick. He said I could learn how to be a knight much better there than at home. At first it was terrible because I missed my mother. But there were three other boys who also wanted to become knights, so it wasn't too bad.

Tasks: Professional warriors and their pay

1 Make a list of key facts about a knight (job, training, weapons, pay).

2 What did a knight have to learn? Right or wrong? Tell your partner.
A knight had to learn:
- to read and write
- to ride a horse in full armour[16]
- to use swords and lances
- to carry a shield
- to use a crossbow (see picture on p. 11)
- to wear helmets and chaincoat
- to cook.

1 warrior *Krieger/in*
2 century *Jahrhundert*
3 to attack *angreifen*
4 fight, fought, fought *kämpfen*
5 knight *Ritter*
6 weapon *Waffe*
7 the pay *die Bezahlung*
8 theory *Theorie*
9 emperor *Kaiser*
10 battle *Kampf*
11 sword *Schwert*
12 lance *Lanze*
13 helmet *Helm*
14 chaincoat *Kettenhemd*
15 shield *Waffenschild*
16 armour *Rüstung*

Noble men and women and their life in castles

S 15 Medieval clothes, 1310–1340

The clothes of noble men and woman were often made of velvet[1] in bright[2] colours. This showed that they were noble and wealthy[3] because the dyes[4] were expensive. Often it was forbidden[5] for other people to wear such clothes.

S 16 Extract[6] from a letter about the life in a castle written by the knight Ulrich von Hutten, 25 October 1518

Die Burg selbst, ob sie auf dem Berg oder in der Ebene liegt, ist nicht als angenehmer Aufenthalt, sondern als Festung gebaut. Sie ist von Mauern und Gräben umgeben, innen ist sie eng und durch Stallungen für Vieh und Pferde zusammengedrängt. Daneben liegen dunkle Kammern, vollgepfropft mit Geschützen, Pech, Schwefel und sonstigem Zubehör für Waffen und Kriegsgerät. Überall stinkt es nach Schießpulver; und dann die Hunde und ihr Dreck ...! Reiter kommen und gehen, darunter Räuber, Diebe und Wegelagerer. Denn fast für alle stehen unsere Häuser offen, weil wir nicht wissen, was das für Leute sind, oder uns nicht groß danach erkundigen.
Man hört das Blöken der Schafe, das Brüllen der Rinder, das Bellen der Hunde, das Rufen der auf dem Feld Arbeitenden, das Knarren und Rattern der Fuhrwerke und Karren; ja sogar das Heulen der Wölfe hört man in unserem Haus, weil es nahe am Wald liegt.

From: Ulrich von Hutten an den Nürnberger Patrizier Willibald Pirckheimer, in: Arno Borst (ed.), Lebensformen im Mittelalter, Frankfurt a.M. 1973, pp. 173–75

Tasks: Life of noble men and women

1 In his letter, Ulrich von Hutten describes many details about life in a castle. Tell your partner what is correct.
- There is not enough room for everybody.
- It is built to be a nice place to live in.
- It is built to be a fortress.
- Everybody is welcome.
- The air is good because the castle is close to the forest.
- It is clean in the castle.
- There is a lot of noise: from the animals, the carts coming in, and from the wolves.
- The weapons are stored in the castle next to where people live.

2 Make a list of the key facts about noble men and women. Before you do this task, have a look at **S 7** on p. 8 and read the information on p. 9.

Key facts about noble men and women

Who were they married to?	*Another noble person*
What type of food did they eat?	...
Where did they live?	...
What clothes did they wear?	...
What work did they do?	
What else may be important?	

Key terms

Noble men and women

Noble men and women belonged to a group of people which was called the nobility[7]. They were noble because their parents were noble too.
In the Middle Ages, their noble birth decided[8] everything for them:
- who they married
- what type of food they ate
- where they lived
- what clothes they wore and
- what work they did.

They stayed in this group all their life.
They had special rights: for example, they were the only ones who were allowed to hunt[9]. The men all trained to be warriors or became churchmen[10].

1 velvet *Samt*
2 bright *hell, leuchtend*
3 wealthy *reich*
4 dye *Farbstoffe*
5 to forbid, forbade, forbidden *verbieten*
6 extract *Auszug*
7 nobility *Adel*
8 to decide (sich) *entscheiden*
9 to hunt *jagen*
10 churchman *Geistlicher*

1.5 Life in a medieval village

Europe is divided into manors[1]

Europe, outside the towns, was a land of **manors**. That meant that a noble **lord**[2] owned all of the land in and around a medieval village with its fields, the pastures[3] and the woodland. The lord could be, for example, the count of Hochstaden, the knight von Hutten, or the abbot[4] of Prüm monastery[5]. The highest lords had sometimes hundreds of manors; the lowliest[6] lords, perhaps only one with twenty peasants. This was just enough to support[7] one knight's family.
But the lords did not only own the land, they also had the right to rule[8] over the peasants who lived on this land. That meant, for example, that the peasants had to ask their lords first if they wanted to leave the village. The lord also was the judge[9] over his peasants.

Nobody is equal

The lords did not work on the land themselves. Peasants did that for them. The lords also had men, called **reeves**[10], who made sure that the **peasants** did their work correctly.
The biggest group of peasants was called ▸ **villeins**[11]. Their lords gave them land, which they could farm for themselves. For that, they had to work on the lords' fields and do other things for them. Another group was made up of men and women without land. They worked on their lords' land or castle and lived in their lords' homes.
All the peasants in the village shared[12] pastures for their animals, a well, and the woodlands. They all also had the right to take some wood from the forest for building, heating and cooking. The peasants' pigs ran free in the forests and ate acorns[13] and other foods.
How much each peasant family had to give or work for their lords was often very different for each family.

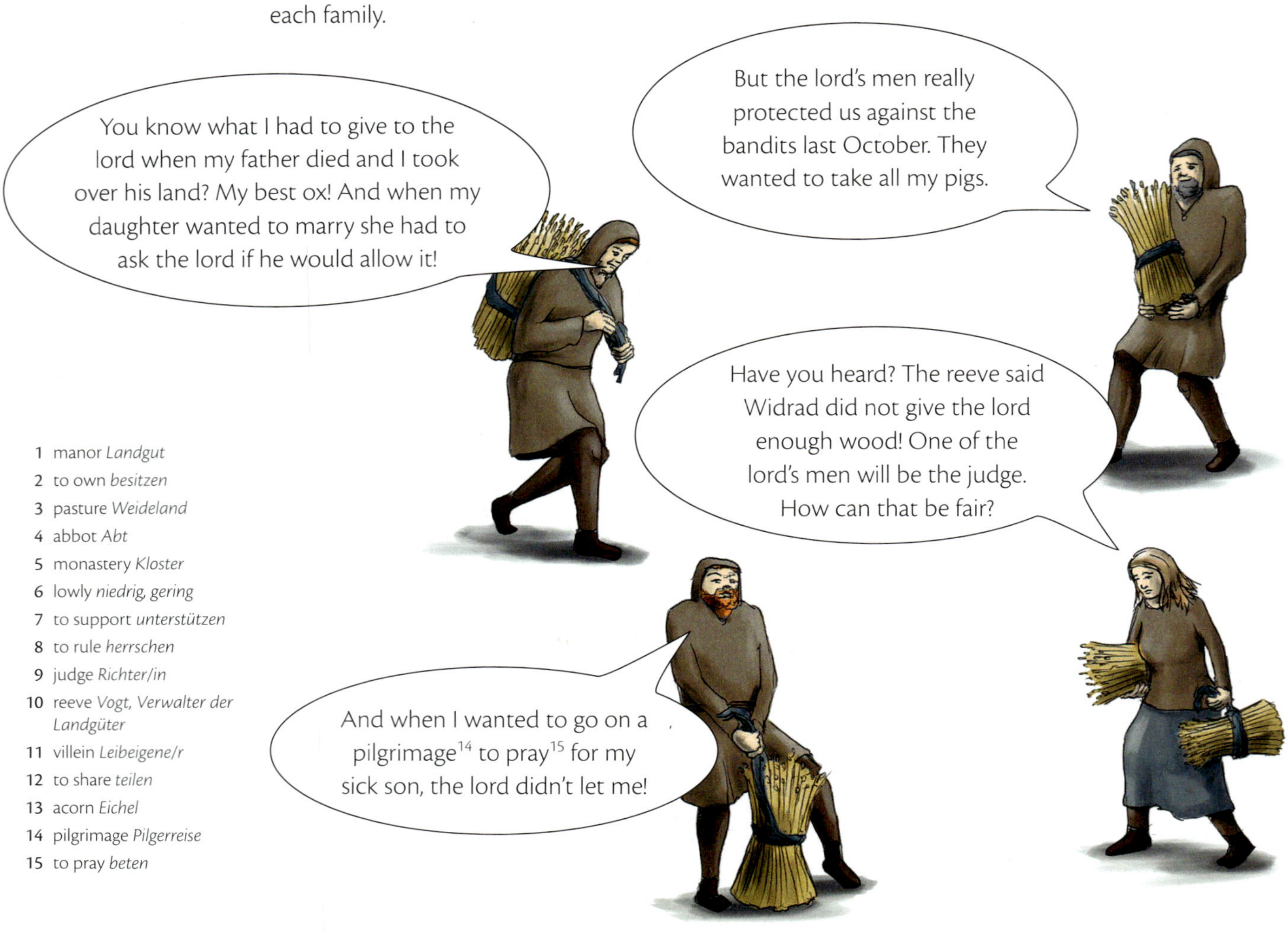

1 manor *Landgut*
2 to own *besitzen*
3 pasture *Weideland*
4 abbot *Abt*
5 monastery *Kloster*
6 lowly *niedrig, gering*
7 to support *unterstützen*
8 to rule *herrschen*
9 judge *Richter/in*
10 reeve *Vogt, Verwalter der Landgüter*
11 villein *Leibeigene/r*
12 to share *teilen*
13 acorn *Eichel*
14 pilgrimage *Pilgerreise*
15 to pray *beten*

S 17 Account[1] of a villein

In 881, the Vikings looted[2] the wealthy Prüm Monastery (today on the border to Belgium in the Eifel, Rhineland-Palatinate[3]). In 893, the abbot of the monastery listed its many manors in what are today Holland, France, Belgium, Luxemburg and Germany. Seven kilometres away from Prüm, the monastery had a manor called Rommersheim, where 30 villeins lived. One of the villeins was Widrad and his family.

Widrad gibt an das Kloster jedes Jahr 1 Eber, 1 Pfund Garn, drei Hühner, 18 Eier.

Er fährt 5 Wagenladungen von seinem Mist auf unsere Äcker, bringt 5 Bündel Baumrinde für die Beleuchtung und fährt 12 Wagenladungen Holz zum Kloster. Dieses Holz dient im Winter zum Heizen. Ferner liefert Widrad dem Kloster jährlich 50 Latten und 100 Schindeln für Dachreparaturen.

Sein Brot bäckt Widrad in unserem Backhaus, und das Bier braut er in unserem Brauhaus. Hierfür zahlt er an das Kloster eine Gebühr.

Eine Woche in jedem Jahr verrichtet er den Hirtendienst bei unserer Schweineherde im Wald. Er bestellt drei Morgen Land, das ganze Jahr hindurch, jede Woche drei Tage.

Bis zum Dezember, wenn das Getreide gedroschen wird, muss er es zusammen mit anderen Hörigen bewachen, damit es nicht von Brandstiftern angezündet wird. Wachdienst muss ebenfalls geleistet werden, wenn der Herr Abt kommt, um ihn vor nächtlicher Gefahr zu beschützen. Wenn Widrad 15 Nächte den Wachdienst verrichtet, das Heu geerntet und auf unseren Äckern gepflügt hat, erhält er in einem guten Erntejahr Brot, Bier und Fleisch; in anderen Jahren erhält er nichts. Die Frau Widrads muss leinene Tücher anfertigen. Sie fertigt daraus Hosen für die Mönche an.

From: Günther Franz, Quellen zur Geschichte des Bauernstandes im Mittelalter. Darmstadt 1967, p. 82 ff.

Tasks: Widrad and his duties[4]

1 The abbot of Prüm monastery asks his reeve about Widrad's duties. Answer his questions.

a How often does Widrad work on our fields?

b Does he have to herd[5] our horses?

c Does his wife make linen cloth[6] and shirts for us?

d Does he have to guard[7] me when I go to Rommersheim?

e How many eggs does he give us and how often?

f He says that he doesn't have to give me any pigs. Is that correct?

1 account *hier: Bericht*
2 to loot *plündern*
3 Rhineland-Palatinate *Rheinland-Pfalz*
4 duty *Pflicht, Aufgabe*
5 to herd cattle *Vieh hüten*
6 cloth *Tuch*
7 to guard *bewachen*
8 book illumination *Buchmalerei*

S 18 ▸ Book illumination[8] from the Queen Mary Psalter, 1310–20

Language help: a sickle to cut grain

2 Pair work. Partner A = the abbot's reeve in Rommersheim; partner B = Widrad. Widrad is not happy with his situation. Write a dialogue. Widrad asks the reeve why he must do all these duties. ***Language help:*** *pay when my wife uses the bakehouse; only get bread, beer and meat for my hard work in good harvest years; have to protect the fields of the monastery.*

3 Write a caption for **S 18**.

Analysing[1] historical objects

When historians want to find out what happened at a certain time in the past[2], they study everything that was created[3] at that time. Studying history means studying the past through things like letters, newspapers, maps, books, photographs, pictures, objects[4] and films. They are all called ▸ **sources**[5].

In museums, you find many of the things which are left from the Middle Ages, like objects which people used in their household, weapons[6] and money. They are just as important for the study of history as written documents or pictures. Each object has a story to tell.
When historians analyse historical objects, they begin with the basic "facts": age, material, location, etc. Then they try to find out what this object tells us about the time when it was made:

- what people ate
- what people did to look good
- how people tried to attack others
- how people produced the things which they needed, etc.

Not all questions can be answered for all objects because some facts are not known.

S 19 **Double-sided comb[7] with a jousting scene[8], 10th century**

This comb is from the Byzantine Empire and made of ivory[9].

Tasks: Historical objects from the Middle Ages

1 Visit a museum which shows objects from the Middle Ages. Find an object which is interesting to you. Take a picture or buy a postcard. The museums often have brochures with information on the object. Write a short text about the object. Use the text on p. 17 as an example.
If you do not find anything, you can use the objects on p. 17.

1 to analyse *analysieren*
2 past *Vergangenheit*
3 to create *schaffen, erstellen*
4 object *Objekt, Gegenstand*
5 source *Quelle*
6 weapon *Waffe*
7 comb *Kamm*
8 jousting scene *Turnierszene*
9 ivory *Elfenbein*

The double-sided comb: Basic facts

The object in the photo on p. 16 is a comb which was made in the ▸ **Byzantine Empire** (*Byzantinisches Reich*) in the 10th century. It can now be found in the *Germanisches Nationalmuseum* in Nuremberg (*Nürnberg*). It is a double-sided comb, which means that you can comb your hair with both sides. It is twelve centimetres long and 10.5 (ten point five) centimetres high. The comb is made of ivory from the tusks[1] of an elephant. In the centre of the comb you see two riders who are riding towards each other. They both have a lance in their hands and are trying to hit each other.

History skills	Activate your English
What is the object made of? How big is it?	*... is made of ...*
Where is the object now?	*... is now in ...*
Who made the object?	*... was made by ...*
Where and when was it created/made?	*... in (place) in/around/circa (time)*
Who was it made for? Who used it or owned it?	*... was made for (name)* *... was owned/used by ...*
How was the object used?	*... was used to ...*
What does the object tell us about the time it was created?	*It proves that ...* *It shows ...*

What does the object tell us about the time it was created?

The price of the comb is not known, but the person who bought it must have paid a high price. Maybe the owner[2] did not use it every day. It is finely made and the material for the comb came from Africa. It was made in the Byzantine Empire and somehow came into the hands of a person in Germany. That proves[3] that expensive goods[4] were traded[5] over long distances.

S 20 Armour[6] for a horse, ca. 1490

This armour from Southern Germany is made of iron[7] and weighs three kilos.

S 21 Elephant Candlestick[8], 13th century

This candlestick is from Magdeburg and made of bronze.

1 tusk *Stoßzahn*
2 owner *Besitzer/in*
3 to prove *beweisen, belegen*
4 goods *Waren, Güter*
5 to trade *handeln*
6 armour *Rüstung*
7 iron *Eisen*
8 candlestick *Kerzenhalter*

1.6 Life in a medieval monastery

S 22 **A young boy is taken into a monastery, book illumination, 1473**

The fictional[1] story of Brother Immo:

Hello, my name is Brother Immo. I came to the monastery 23 years ago when I was seven. My family owns a lot of manors not very far from here. I am the youngest of four brothers and three sisters. Of course, it was clear that I would never inherit[2] any land. Only my oldest brother did when my father died.
I'm content[3] with my life here, although[4] it is hard. I'm not allowed to marry or have children. I only eat the simplest food and I only eat meat on important feast days[5] like at Christmas. Usually, I spend my time praying[6] and working inside. I'm the one who writes down what is happening. The abbot told me that my handwriting is the best. Sometimes I copy old books. Last year I copied a prayer book[7] with beautiful pictures for the wife of the count of Hochstaden. She gave the monastery four oxen for that. My abbot was very happy then.
My best friend, Brother Reginhart, makes sure that the peasants give us what they have to. Then he makes sure that the monastery sends two horses and three lances to the King because that is what we have to do each year. And when someone in his family wants to pray here in our church, we have to accept them as our guests for as long as they want to stay. Last year, the King's mother came here with her servants and 5 horses. She became very ill and so she stayed for three months. They ate a lot of our food. We were lucky because the next harvest was very good.
All the monks[8] have to work. Everybody has to do something. We have a small hospital where Brother Grimald cares for the sick. Brother Ludwig teaches the young boys who come here to become monks. Others welcome the travellers who need some food and a place to stay for the night because there is no other place for them. We also have a brother here who makes the most beautiful objects for the church. My abbot says we need them to praise[9] our Lord Jesus.
My abbot travels a lot. He often spends time checking on[10] our manors, but he also spends time with the King and the King's nobles. The King needs the abbots and other churchmen to run the country[11] because they are the only ones who can read and write.
We monks believe that we lead[12] good Christian lives. I'm sure we will get our reward[13] for that in heaven[14]. But we pray for all people outside the monastery too: for the peasants and the lords. The lords and their wives sometimes give us something for our prayers: land or other things. They think it will help them to go to heaven.

1 fictional *fiktional, erfunden*
2 to inherit sth. *etw. erben*
3 content (adj.) *zufrieden*
4 although *obwohl*
5 feast day *Feiertag*
6 to pray *beten*
7 prayer book *Gebetsbuch*
8 monk *Mönch*
9 to praise *loben, lobpreisen*
10 to check on sth. *etw. kontrollieren*
11 to run the country *das Land regieren*
12 to lead, led, led *führen*
13 reward *Belohnung*
14 heaven *(biblischer) Himmel*

S 23

S 24

S 25

S 26

S 27

S 28

Task: Life in the monastery

Match the captions **a–g** to the correct pictures **S 22–28**.

a This picture shows the big room where we all sleep. It is called the dormitory[1]. Fire is not allowed there so it is really cold in winter. We all sleep in our clothes on straw[2] mattresses, but we wear extra warm shoes at night so we can quickly get up and enter the church at midnight.

b Here you see me getting a haircut. All monks get the same haircut. It is called a tonsure[3]. The top of my head is shaved[4]. You can see what it looks like in the other pictures.

c This is the cup, which one of my brothers made for the wine we drink at ▸ **Holy Communion**[5].

d Here is a picture of me when my father gave me to the monks at the monastery near our castle. Can you imagine how I felt? My father told me that I would never be strong enough to be a knight. He wanted the monks to take care of me and educate[6] me so that I can also become a monk when I grow up.

e Here you can see the monk who is responsible for the wine making. He likes to be in the cellar all by himself. I think I know why.

f At harvest time, we all have to help. I can tell you working in the fields with a sickle is hard work. That's why I do not look too happy in that picture.

g This picture shows me with my very strict teacher. I was really afraid of him. When I could not remember all the Latin words fast enough, he hit me.

1 dormitory *Schlafsaal*
2 straw *Stroh*
3 tonsure *Tonsur, geschorene Haare*
4 to shave *rasieren*
5 Holy Communion *Heilige Kommunion*
6 to educate *erziehen, ausbilden*

S 29 Plan of a typical monastery

S 30 My daily routine[1] in summer

1.45 a.m.[2] Wake up
2.00 a.m. Church service
3.30 a.m. Sleep
4.00 a.m. Church service
5.00 a.m. Private reading and prayer
6.00 a.m. Church service then breakfast
7.00 a.m. Work
8.00 a.m. Church service
9.15 a.m. Work
11.45 a.m. Church service
12.00 p.m.[3] Midday meal
1.00 p.m. Private reading and prayer
1.45 p.m. Sleep
3.00 p.m. Work
5.45 p.m. Meal
6.00 p.m. Church service
7.15 p.m. Private reading and prayer
7.45 p.m. Church service
8.00 p.m. Bed and sleep

S 31 Rules in my monastery

- No one is allowed to argue[4] with the abbot.
- Everybody must do kitchen work.
- One brother always reads the Bible at mealtimes.
- Nobody is allowed to talk during mealtimes.
- Laziness[5] leads to sin[6]. When brothers are not reading or praying, they must work with their hands.
- Monks who come too late to church services will be punished[7].
- Nobody is allowed to own anything.
- Guests are welcome.

My clothes

In the pictures on p. 19, you can see that we monks dress simply. I have two outfits[8] so that I can have something to wear when one outfit is in the wash. They are black and easy to make. These clothes tell everybody that I'm a monk. Nuns[9] dress almost in the same way, but they also put on a veil[10] so you can't see their hair.

1 routine *Routine, Tagesablauf*
2 a.m. = ante meridiem / before midday *vormittags*
3 p.m. = post meridiem / after midday *nachmittags*
4 to argue *streiten, argumentieren*
5 laziness *Faulheit*
6 sin *Sünde*
7 to punish *bestrafen*
8 outfit *Bekleidung*
9 nun *Nonne*
10 veil *Schleier*

Tasks: The life of a monk

1 Make a list of all the ways the life of a monk was easy (pp. 18–20).
2 Make a list of all the ways the life of a monk was hard.
3 Give possible reasons why many monasteries became very rich.

1.7 Everybody had to lead a good Christian life

All people wanted to lead a Christian life because most were afraid of what would happen to them if they did not. Their priests told them that there were a lot of things which they could do wrong, for example, not going to church on Sunday, swearing[1], and gambling[2]. The Church taught that life went on after the body had died. People knew that if they did something wrong, they would be punished not only here on earth, but also after their body had died.

Pictures in churches showed people the punishment (**S 32**). They would suffer[3] forever[4].

S 32 **Fra Angelico, "Hell"[5], painting, ca. 1431**

The devil[6] is chewing[7] on some naked souls[8]; others are boiling[9] in hot water. A demon[10] is pouring[11] gold into a pot to melt[12] it. Another is pouring melted gold into the mouth of a soul as a snake strangles[13] him.

But the Church also gave people hope. Priests taught people what they could do to go to heaven. The priests could also forgive[14] their sins[15]. That helped to make the time in purgatory (*Fegefeuer*) shorter. Purgatory was the place where the soul stayed until all the sins had been burned away. Then the soul went to heaven.

Key terms

The Medieval Church

You know already that a church is a building where Christians go on Sunday for the church service, but it can also mean the organisation to which all Christians belong. In the Middle Ages, everybody belonged to the Catholic Church. The head[16] of the Catholic Church is the Pope, below him are archbishops, bishops, abbots and then the priests. The men who are working for the Church are called "churchmen". Women can only become nuns. The peasants had to pay a tax[17] to the Church called the ▸ **tithe**[18].

Tasks: The Church and its idea of hell

1 Give possible reasons[19] why the Church made the people so afraid of going to hell.

2 The devil is pouring gold into a man's mouth (**S 32**). What do you think the man has done wrong?

1 to swear, swore, sworn *hier: fluchen*
2 to gamble *um Geld spielen*
3 to suffer *leiden*
4 forever *für immer, ewig*
5 hell *Hölle*
6 devil *Teufel*
7 to chew *kauen*
8 soul *Seele*
9 to boil *kochen*
10 demon *Dämon*
11 to pour *gießen*
12 to melt *schmilzen, schmelzen*
13 to strangle *erwürgen*
14 to forgive, forgave, forgiven *vergeben*
15 sin *Sünde*
16 head *hier: Oberhaupt*
17 tax *Steuer*
18 tithe *Zehnte*
19 reason *Grund*

1.8 Life in a medieval town

S 33 **The town of Monteriggioni in Italy still looks like a typical medieval town.**

Around 1300, Germany changed. A traveller saw more towns with walls around them, with a market and a church in the middle. They must have looked a lot like Monteriggioni in Italy still looks today.

S 34 **Map of Aalen (Baden-Württemberg) in 1528**

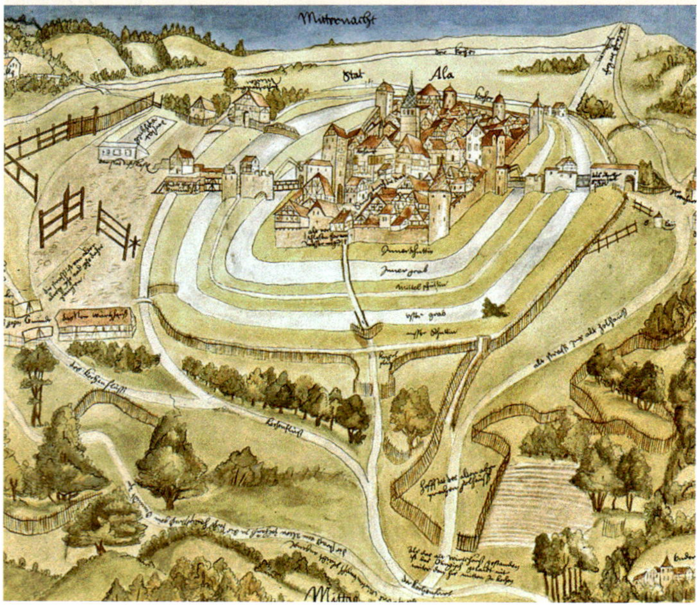

Medieval market towns

In the century before, many lords had bought goods[1] which travelling **merchants**[2] had brought from Italy and other places. These merchants only stopped at places where they were safe from attacks. The noble lords founded **market places** which were under their protection[3]. They built them at places where a lot of people met or where it was easy to defend[4] them: at crossroads[5], near a place to cross a river, near a castle or close to a monastery. Towns also had to be near a river because towns needed more water than villages. The different craftsmen[6] also needed the water for their work.

Deep ditches[7] and strong walls were built around the towns to protect the townspeople from attack. Strong gatehouses[8] around the walls with drawbridges gave extra protection. At night, the towns raised[9] the drawbridges and shut the gates[10].

1 goods *Waren, Güter*
2 merchant *Kaufmann*
3 protection *Schutz*
4 to defend *verteidigen*
5 crossroad *Kreuzung*
6 craftsman *Handwerker*
7 ditch *Graben*
8 gatehouse *Wachturm*
9 to raise *hochziehen*
10 gate *Stadttor*

S 35 **The duke of Zähringen founded the town of Freiburg (today in Baden-Württemberg, near the French border) in 1120.**

Es sei bekannt, dass ich, Konrad (Herzog von Zähringen), auf meinem eigenen Besitz, im Jahre des Herrn 1120 einen Markt (Freiburg) eingerichtet habe. Nachdem ich Kaufleute der Umgebung zusammengerufen habe, habe ich beschlossen, diesen Markt zu gründen und einzurichten. Jedem Kaufmann habe ich ein Hausgrundstück zu eigen gegeben und bestimmt, dass von jedem dieser Grundstücke pro Jahr ein Schilling Zins [Pachtgebühren] gezahlt werden soll...

1. Allen denen, die zu meinem Markt kommen, gewähre ich Frieden und Schutz...

3. Allen Kaufleuten der Stadt wird der Zoll erlassen...

4. Den Bürgern will ich keinen anderen Richter und Priester geben als den, welchen sie sich selbst erwählt haben...

5. Wenn ein Streit oder Rechtsfall entsteht, soll nicht von mir und meinen Richtern darüber entschieden werden, sondern nach Gewohnheit und Recht aller Kaufleute, wie sie besonders in Köln geübt werden ...

6. Wer über Jahr und Tag in der Stadt gewohnt hat, ohne dass irgendein Herr ihn als seinen Leibeigenen gefordert hat, der genießt von da an sicher die Freiheit.

From: Dieter Starke, Herrschaft und Genossenschaft im Mittelalter, Stuttgart 1971, p. 86ff.

S 36 **A villein has made it into the town of Freiburg.**

Tasks: The founding of Freiburg (S 35)

1 Right or wrong? Tell your partner.
- Everybody who came to the market had to protect himself.
- Every merchant had to pay different rent[1] for the land which his house stood on.
- Merchants did not have to pay customs duties[2].
- The townspeople elected[3] their own judge and priest.
- A villein who had lived in Freiburg for a short time would be free.

2 How did the Count of Zähringen try to make Freiburg attractive[4] to merchants? Right or wrong? Tell your partner.
He promised[5] them
- the freedom[6] to choose their own judge.
- the freedom to choose their religion.
- protection against bandits when they were travelling.
- a higher income[7].

3 The Count promised a lot to the merchants to make Freiburg attractive to them. Give reasons why he did that. What were the advantages[8] for him? ***Language help***: *The text says that ... It is also possible that ...*

4 Describe the scene in the modern illustration (**S 36**). Before you do this, answer the following questions:
a Who is the man in green and the man in red?
b Why does the man in green say: "Thank God! I made it!" What does it mean?
c Where does the scene take place?

5 In the evening, the man in red comes home. He tells his wife what he has been doing that day. Tell his story.

6 The man in green is asked: "What are you doing here?" Give his answer.

1 rent *Miete*
2 customs duties *Zollabgaben*
3 to elect *wählen*
4 attractive *reizvoll, anziehend*
5 to promise *versprechen*
6 freedom *Freiheit*
7 income *Einkommen*
8 advantage *Vorteil*

S 37 Pyramid of estates *(Ständepyramide)*

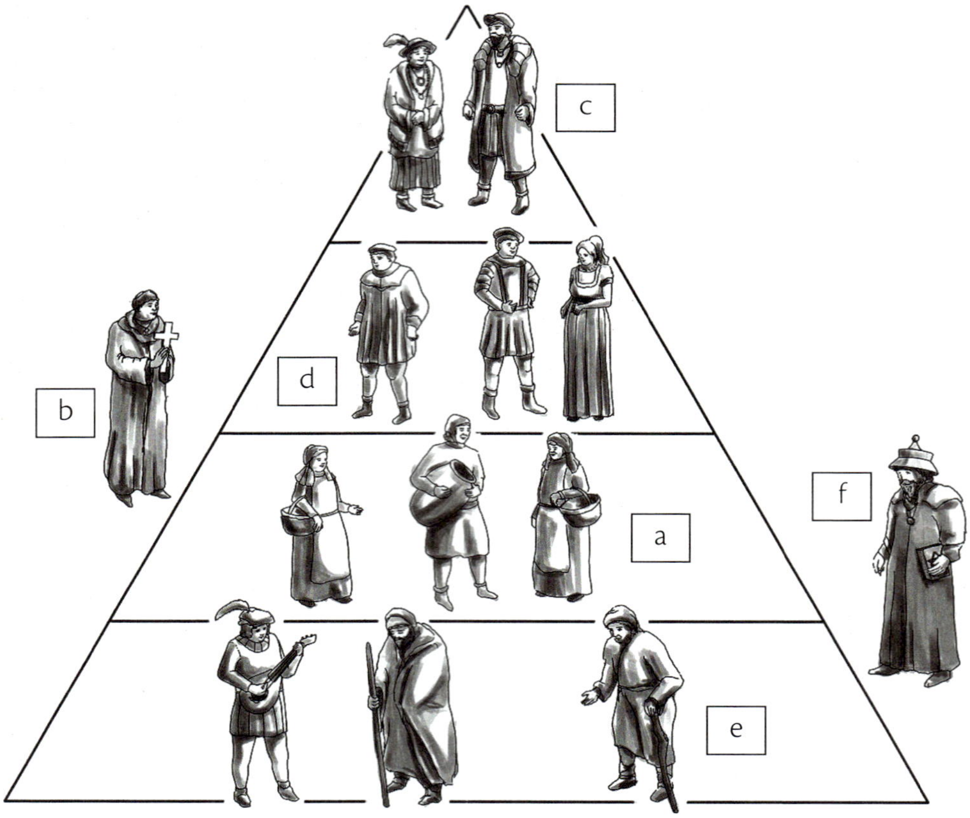

Who lived in the towns?

1 The long-distance merchants[1] had their beautiful stone houses on their own land around the market place. They brought goods from Italy to the German towns. They had the highest rank[2] in the towns. They were called "patricians" *(Patrizier)*. Usually, people could only be a member[3] of this group if they were the child of a patrician family or if they married a patrician. They were the smallest group, but patricians were the ones who ruled the towns.

2 ▸ Jewish people[4] had to live in special areas of the towns called ghettos[5], which they could only leave during the day. They had to wear special clothes and they were not allowed to become members of the guilds[6] of the craftsmen. Most of them worked as moneylenders[7] or peddlers[8]. Again and again, Christians attacked Jews. They were not counted as full citizens[9].

3 The "dishonest[10] **or unclean people"** were at the bottom[11] of society[12] in the towns: people who worked with dead bodies like hangmen[13], knackers[14] and gravediggers[15], people who were ill, people who had no money or job (beggars[16]), and people who travelled from town to town and entertained people like musicians. They were not counted as full citizens.

4 The master[17] **craftsmen,** who owned their own workshops[18], had the second highest rank in the towns. They fought with the patricians about their right to have a say in the towns. The master craftsmen formed guilds. Each craft[19] (bakers, butchers, cloth[20] makers, carpenters, candle makers, etc.) had its own guild. They had their workshops and their shops in the same street (e.g. *Bäckergasse*). Guild members helped each other, for example, when someone was sick. The town guilds were the big rule[21] makers. Guilds decided who was allowed to work at

1 long-distance merchant *Fernhandelskaufmann*
2 rank *Rang, Stellung*
3 member *Mitglied*
4 Jewish people *Juden*
5 ghetto *Ghetto*
6 guilds *Zunft*
7 moneylender *Geldverleiher/in*
8 peddler *Hausierer/in*
9 citizen *Bürger/in*
10 dishonest *unehrlich*
12 society *Gesellschaft*
11 at the bottom *hier: am unteren Ende*
13 hangman *Henker*
14 knacker *Abdecker; jmd., der Tierkadaver beseitigt*
15 gravedigger *Totengräber*
16 beggar *Bettler/in*
17 master *Handwerksmeister/in*
18 workshop *Werkstatt*
19 craft *Handwerk*
20 cloth *Tuch*
21 rule *Regel*

S 38–40 **Scenes of life in a medieval town, book illuminations, Jean Bourdichon, 1505–10**

a craft and you did not have a chance to work at a craft if you did not belong to the guild. A guild was great – as long as you were in one.

5 **The many apprentices**[1]**, journeymen**[2]**, innkeepers**[3] **and servants** who were working and living in the town did not have a say in anything. They were not counted[4] as citizens. They could not buy any land in the town. If you wanted to learn a craft you had to become an apprentice, usually for seven years. Then you could become a journeyman. After another seven years you could become a master, but only if you produced a perfect piece of work. Then you could become a citizen.

6 **Many priests**[5]**, monks and nuns**[6] also lived in the towns, but they were not citizens. In some cities, only 20 per cent of the population were citizens. Priests, monks and nuns lived by their own Church rules and laws.

Tasks: Life in medieval towns

1 Anno, a young villein, is happy now. He has reached the town of Freiburg (**S 36**). He knows that he will only be free if his lord, the abbot of Prüm monastery, will not find him or ask for him in the next year.
What can he do to earn[7] some money? Does he have the chance to become a citizen?
Give possible ways how he can make a living and become a citizen.

2 Match the texts 1–6 on pp. 24-25 to the letters a–f in the diagram (**S 37**) on p. 24?

3 Write captions for the sources **S 38–40**.

4 In many towns, there were conflicts between the different groups. Give possible reasons why they were fighting against each other and what they were fighting for.

1 apprentice *Lehrling*
2 journeyman *Handwerks-geselle*
3 innkeeper *Gastwirt/in*
4 to count *zählen*
5 priest *Priester*
6 nun *Nonne*
7 to earn sth. *etw. verdienen*

Who ruled the town?

At the beginning, local lords ruled most towns. When the towns became richer, they could buy their freedom. Others only won their freedom after some fights with their lords. Some towns like Freiburg were free from the beginning.

The towns had their own government[1], which was called "**town council**"[2] (*Rat der Stadt*). At first, only the wealthy long-distance merchants were members of the town council but after some fights, **master craftsmen** could also be in it. The **long-distance merchants** and the master craftsmen were also the only **full citizens** (*Vollbürger*) in their town. They were the only ones who elected the members of the town council.

Sometimes only 20 per cent of the population were full citizens. That meant that most people had no say[3] as to how the town government worked.

The town council decided

The town council made laws about every aspect of town life: for example, wandering pigs in the streets, prices, safety of the citizens and the quality of the products which were made or sold in the towns.

S 41 **The Town of London, 1364**

John Penrose has sold wine which was bad. He must drink a lot of his own bad wine. The rest of the wine will be poured over his head.

From: Byrom, Jamie / Counsell, Christine / Riley, Michael, Medieval Minds. Britain 1066–1500, Harlow 1997, p. 34

S 42 **The Town of York, 1301**

Fish must not be sold after the evening church service or before the first church service.

From: Byrom, Jamie / Consell, Christine / Riley, Michael, Medieval Minds. Britain 1066–1500, Harlow 1997, p. 34

S 43 **The town of Landshut in Bavaria, 1256**

Wir verbieten, Schwerter innerhalb der Stadt zu tragen.
Und wenn Leute getroffen werden, die Schwerter tragen, werden sie der Stadt eine hohe Strafe zahlen.

From: Landshuter Markt- und Gewerbeordnung von 1256

S 44 **The Town of Norwich, 1423**

Townspeople must form a group to patrol[4] the town at night. Anyone who does not do that has to pay a fine[5]. All the men of the town must help to put out burning houses.

From: Norman Pounds, The Medieval City, Westport 2005

1 government *Regierung*
2 council *Rat*
3 to have a say *etw. zu sagen haben, etw. bestimmen*
4 to patrol *patrouillieren*
5 fine (n) *Strafgebühr*

Task: Town government

1 Explain why each law was made. Why was it forbidden, for example, to sell fish at night?
2 Give a definition of a "full citizen" in the medieval town.

The towns stank

Medieval towns were small, dirty and smelly. Streets were narrow[1], about two to three metres wide, and not paved[2]. Pigs, dogs and rats looked for things to eat in the streets. Finding something was easy because people threw their rubbish into the streets.

Medieval towns did not have systems of sewers[3]. Waste water[4] flowed down the street and then into a stream[5] or river. Drinking water was pumped up from public[6] wells[7] or came from the streams and rivers. The houses did not have bathrooms so people used public bathhouses. They also used public latrines[8] (= toilets), which were emptied into the river too. Sometimes the contents[9] of the latrines were used as manure[10] for the vegetable gardens outside the town walls.

The town laws demanded[11] that people cleaned up the street in front of their houses, but many sources tell us that much of the rubbish stayed in the streets.

S 45 Street scene in a medieval town, 1476

The towns were dangerous

With so many people living so close together, illnesses[12] spread[13] easily. Many people slept in the same room or bed. Their lice[14] carried their illnesses (for example, typhus[15]) to the person who was sleeping next to them. Drinking the water from the rivers made people ill too so people liked to drink beer since[16] it was cleaner.

Houses were expensive because the number of people grew quickly, but not the town because it was expensive to build new walls. Houses usually had several floors and were built as closely together as possible. Most houses were made of wood and their roofs[17] of straw. That is why people were afraid of fires which could destroy[18] all the houses in one street in a short time. Little could be done against such fires. In the evening and at night it was totally dark in the streets. There were no street lights. People who had to go somewhere at night took along lanterns and it was a very good idea to have a strong person with them!

Tasks: Life in towns is hard

1 Make a list of all the ways the life of a townsperson was hard.

2 Make a list of the reasons why a villein wanted to live in a town.

3 What is the same – what is different? Copy and fill in the table and find out how the modern illustration of a medieval town (**S 45**) is different from or the same as the description of a medieval town above.

	Modern illustration	*Text description above*
streets	*not paved, …*	
…		
houses		*built as closely together as possible*
…		
	…	

1 narrow *eng, schmal*
2 to pave *pflastern, befestigen*
3 system of sewers *Kanalsystem, Kanalisation*
4 waste water *Abwasser*
5 stream *Strom, Bach*
6 public *öffentlich*
7 well *Quelle, Pumpe*
8 latrine *Latrine*
9 content *Inhalt*
10 manure *Dünger*
11 to demand *verlangen, fordern*
12 illness *Krankheit*
13 to spread, spread, spread *sich ausbreiten*
14 lice *Läuse*
15 typhus *Fleckfieber*
16 since *hier: weil*
17 roof *Dach*
18 to destroy *zerstören*

A woman's work is never done: Three women's fictional stories

S 46 The sister on the right with the red prayer book – that's me. Like in the men's monasteries, we have seven church services a day. I'm **Sister Imelda**. I am one of Brother Immo's older sisters. I came to this convent[1] when I was ten because I wanted to lead a true Christian life. At that time, my oldest sister had just died having her first child. She was only 15. Giving birth[2] can be very dangerous. The year before her death, she had married Benno. My father and his father thought it was a good idea to be one family since relatives[3] always help each other. They did not ask my sister or Benno what they wanted. Parents always decide. I did not want this for myself so I asked my father if I could enter a convent. After some months, he finally agreed[4]. Not many women are allowed to do this and many are not able to since they do not have the land or money, which they have to give to the convent before entering. In the convent, I have to work. With some other sisters, I make the beautiful clothes for our bishop.

S 47 That's me with my youngest. I'm making some soup for us. Sometimes it's hard to have enough to eat in the winter. I'm **Berta**. I live in a village with my husband Widrad and our five children. I always get up when the sun rises and start to work. I start the fire, make our porridge[5], take the grain[6] to the mill, care for the vegetable garden, brew the beer, feed the chicken, make the butter and the cheese, do the spinning[7] and weaving[8] and sew[9] the clothes. What I hate most is washing the clothes in the cold river. What I like best is baking bread in the village bakehouse because I meet other women there. We always have something to talk about. Although the children help as much as they can, I am always tired. I must not complain[10]. My children are alive, the harvests have been good and we always have enough to eat.

S 48 The man in the middle is my husband. Peter is on the right. On the left is Conrad, our apprentice. Here they are hammering a piece of iron. The baker Hans wanted to have a new shop sign. I'm **Anna**. I live in a big town. My husband died six months ago. He was a master in the blacksmith[11] guild. I have always been a good housewife, but I have also always worked in the workshop when my husband needed me. I can make keys just as well as my journeyman Peter. And you should have seen the shield I made last year! The count[12] paid a good price for that. The others in the guild have really helped me a lot after my husband's death. They even paid for his funeral[13], but now they are making trouble. They say that I am a woman and cannot work as a master. It is so unfair. I think I must marry a man in the guild. What about Peter? Next year he will be a master and he doesn't look so bad!

1 convent *Konvent, Kloster*
2 birth *Geburt*
3 relative *Verwandte/r*
4 to agree *zustimmen*
5 porridge *Haferbrei*
6 grain *Korn*
7 to spin *spinnen*
8 to weave *weben*
9 to sew *nähen*
10 to complain *sich beschweren*
11 blacksmith *Schmied*
12 count *Graf*
13 funeral *Bestattung*

Task: Medieval men and women

How were the lives of men and women different from each other? Make a list.

Unit revision

Life in the Middle Ages

Activate your English

Talking and writing about life in the Middle Ages

Key terms

AD • BC • monastery • convent • nobility • warrior • knight • manor • craftsman • merchant • peasant • villein • the Church

History skills

Analysing historical objects

S 49 Three medieval men, book illumination, 13th century

S 50 A typical medieval town today

Revision tasks: Life in the Middle Ages

1 Make a list of the key facts about **a** monks and nuns and **b** villeins. Use the table on p. 13 (noble men and women) as an example.

2 Describe the three men in the 13th century book illumination (**S 49**). Explain who the three men are. How do you know who they are? Explain the possible relationship between the three men.

3 **S 50** shows an ideal medieval town. Make a list of all the ways it was ideal. ***Language help:*** *The town had …*

4 Explain the German saying *Stadtluft macht frei* (The air in towns makes you free).

Unit 2 Pilgrimages and Crusades

2.1 Saying sorry for your sins

S1 Holy[1] Robe[2] of Trier

S2 Modern drawing of a pilgrim

Travelling to holy places in the Middle Ages

In the Middle Ages, many people – men and women, rich and poor – went on short or long journeys[3] to holy places. These journeys are called pilgrimages[4]. People believed that they could see something important there or that something important happened at these holy places. Others had asked a saint to help them in a difficult situation and had promised[5] a pilgrimage to say thank you.

Sometimes Christians walked for one or two days to the shrine of a saint near them; for example, to ▸ **Cologne Cathedral** (*Kölner Dom*) to see and pray at the golden ▸ **Shrine[6] of the Three Kings** (*Schrein der Heiligen Drei Könige*). Other people travelled all the way to ▸ **Rome** in Italy. Those who wanted more and could pay for it went to ▸ **Palestine** (*Palästina*), the Holy Land of the Christians, to see where Jesus had lived and died.

After the pilgrims[7] got there, they went to the church to pray[8]. They believed that God would then forgive[9] them for the wrong things (their sins) which they had done in their life. Or, if they were ill, they prayed to become healthy again.

Muslim people travelled on the *haj*, which many still do nowadays. That is a pilgrimage to ▸ **Mecca** (in modern Saudi Arabia). In Mecca, they pray at the place where they believe ▸ **Mohammed** went up to Heaven[10].

Many sources say that pilgrims had a good time. They met new people, saw new places and had adventures, a little bit like when you go on holidays today.

Activate your English

Talking about events[11] which might have happened:

*Use **'might' or 'may' + have + past participle** to express an opinion about something which happened in the past that you think has a good chance to be true.*

The Pope may have said this to ...

The crusaders might have done it because ...

If you want to express that a reason or event has no chance to be true you can say:

They can't have done that because...

This cannot have happened like this because ...

1 holy *heilig*
2 robe *Mantel, Gewand*
3 journey *Reise*
4 pilgrimage *Pilgerreise, Pilgerschaft*
5 to promise *versprechen*
6 shrine *Heiligenschrein*
7 pilgrims *Pilger (Sg, Pl)*
8 to pray *beten*
9 to forgive *etw. vergeben, verzeihen*
10 heaven *(biblischer) Himmel*
11 event *Ereignis*

Tasks: Travelling to holy places

1 Give a one-minute presentation on pilgrimages. Talk about who went where and give possible reasons why a person may/might have gone on a pilgrimage.

2 Find out whether people still go on pilgrimages today. If so, where do they go?

S3 **Wolves are attacking pilgrims, manuscript, Museum of Roncevalles**

S4 **Travelling in the Middle Ages**

Was travelling fun?

Travellers could choose to walk or to ride on a horse or donkey[1]. They could also travel in a cart[2] or, if they were wealthy[3], in a carriage[4]. That was easiest, but it must have still been very uncomfortable[5] because the roads were not paved[6]. This made travelling in bad weather almost impossible. Laws[7]demanded[8] that landowners[9] repair the broken roads and bridges, but travellers often complained[10] that nobody had done anything. Only very good riders could ride 50 kilometres a day.

Travellers often lost their way because the road signs were wrong or missing. They also had to fear[11] bandits, who would attack[12] and rob[13] them, especially at night. That is why most travellers went in groups.

Finding something to eat and a place for the night was also not simple. They were lucky if they found a monastery[14] which welcomed them. The wealthy people would also stay at an inn[15], if they found one. The poor had to ask people who lived along their way for a safe place for the night.

S5 **An account[16] of a journey from Northamptonshire to London in 1450 (fourteen fifty)**

160 persons and more, all dressed in the form of war with helmets, long swords and other weapons, hid under a large hedge[17] next to the highway. They waited for William Tresham from midnight to six o'clock, when William appeared[18]. They attacked and killed him. And they gave him many more deadly wounds[19] and cut his throat.

From: Shephard, Colin / Corbishley, Mike / Large, Alan / Tames, Richard, Contrasts & Connections. London 1991. p. 104

S6 **Street robbery, book illumination, 1250–1260**

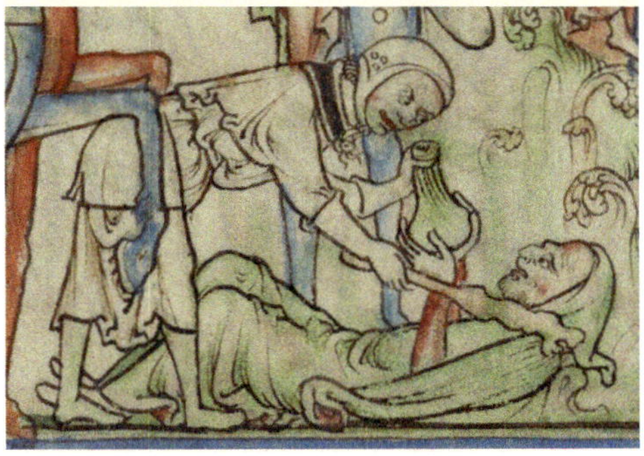

1 donkey *Esel*
2 cart *Karren*
3 wealthy *wohlhabend*
4 carriage *Kutsche*
5 uncomfortable *unbequem, ungemütlich*
6 to pave *befestigen, pflastern*
7 law *Gesetz*
8 to demand *verlangen, fordern*
9 landowner *Landbesitzer*
10 to complain *sich beklagen, beschweren*
11 to fear sth. *etw. fürchten*
12 to attack *angreifen*
13 to rob *ausrauben, rauben*
14 monastery *Kloster*
15 inn *Gasthaus*
16 account *hier: Bericht*
17 hedge *Hecke, Gebüsch*
18 to appear *erscheinen, auftauchen*
19 wound *Wunde*

Tasks: Travelling in the Middle Ages

1 You want to convince your wife/husband that you must go on a long pilgrimage. Write down your arguments. Then write down the arguments which she/he uses to stop you.

2 In 1450, not all the roads in England were safe for travellers. Give possible reasons. ***Language help:*** *Not all the roads were safe because …*

2.2 Winning back Jerusalem

S7 **Urban II is giving a sermon[1] at Clermont in 1095, book illumination**

For many centuries[2], Christians in Europe travelled to ▸ **Jerusalem** in Palestine to visit the places where Jesus had lived and died. Beginning in 637 AD, the city was under the control of Arab[3] Muslims, who allowed the visits. But in the eleventh century, the Turks[4] conquered[5] most of the Byzantine[6] lands in Asia Minor[7] and they made visits to Jerusalem more difficult.

In 1095 (one thousand ninety-five), the Christian Byzantine Emperor[8] sent a letter to the head of the Catholic Church[9], the Pope in Rome. He asked for Christian[10] knights[11] to help him fight the Turks. Five months later in November, at a church meeting in France, ▸ **Pope Urban II** gave a sermon. He asked the French[12] knights to help their Christian brothers in the ▸ **Byzantine Empire**[13] to win back ▸ Palestine with Jerusalem.

S8 **Extract[14] from Urban's sermon**

It was not written down at the time. Years later, five accounts were written down in Latin[15]. Robert of Reims, a French monk[16], wrote down his account 25 years later in 1120.

A ▸ race[17], who does not know God, has come to the lands of the Christians and has killed them. They also destroy[18] churches. You must go and take revenge[19] for that. Jerusalem is at the centre of the world. This royal[20] city is now in the hands of God's[21] enemies[22]. She (= Jerusalem) is the slave[23] of people who do not accept[24] God. She asks you to free her and save her.

All men who go there and die on their journey or in the fights against the heathens[25] will be forgiven their sins.

Until now, you have fought and killed each other. Stop that. Instead[26], save the Holy Land from that unclean race.

From: Dana C. Munro, Urban and the Crusaders. Translations and Reprints from the Original Sources of European History, Vol. 1:2, Philadelphia 1895, pp. 5–8

1 sermon *Predigt*
2 century *Jahrhundert*
3 Arab *Araber/in*
4 Turk *Türke/Türkin*
5 to conquer *erobern*
6 Byzantine *byzantinisch*
7 Asia Minor *Kleinasien*
8 emperor *Kaiser*
9 church *Kirche*
10 Christian *christlich*
11 knight *Ritter*
12 French *französisch*
13 Empire *Reich*
14 extract *Auszug*
15 Latin *Latein*
16 monk *Mönch*
17 race *Rasse, Geschlecht*
18 to destroy *zerstören*
19 to take revenge *Rache üben*
20 royal *königlich*
21 God *Gott*
22 enemy *Feind/in*
23 slave *Sklave/Sklavin*
24 to accept *hinnehmen, akzeptieren*
25 heathen *Heide/Heidin*
26 instead *stattdessen*
27 to criticize *kritisieren*
28 afterwards *hinterher*
29 historian *Historiker/in*
30 to recognize *erkennen, anerkennen*

Tasks: What did Urban say?

1 Sum up what Urban told his listeners in Robert's account. Use your own words as much as possible. The following words will help you do it: to demand, to criticize[27], to promise, to complain. ***Language help:*** *In his sermon, the Pope demands that his listeners …*

2 Urban used the pronoun "she" for the city of Jerusalem showing that for him, the city was like a woman. Give possible reasons why he did that. ***Language help:*** *He called the city of Jerusalem "she" to show … He wanted the knights to …*

3 Imagine you heard the Pope preach. Afterwards[28] you come home and tell your family that you want to go on a crusade. Give your reasons. Put the strongest argument at the end.

4 What does your family say? Write a dialogue and act out the scene in class.

5 Who are the people in **S7**? How can a historian[29] recognize[30] the different persons? ***Language help:*** *The person on the left must be … because … The group of men on the right must be … The men can be recognized because …*

S9 The Byzantine Empire – Europe, Northern Africa and Western Asia ca. 1095

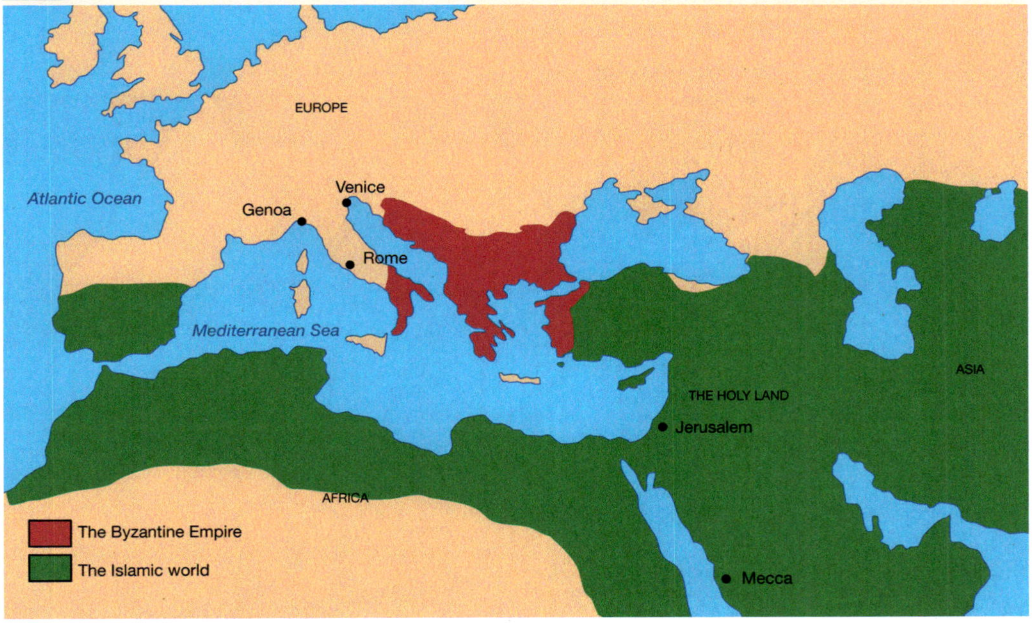

Key terms

Byzantine Empire

The Christian ▸ Byzantine Empire (*Byzantinisches Reich*) ruled[1] most of Eastern and Southern Europe, as well as Asia Minor throughout the Middle Ages[2]. Its capital[3], **Constantinople** (*Konstantinopel*, today ▸ **Istanbul** in Turkey), was the largest and wealthiest city in Europe at the time. Throughout much of the Middle Ages, the Christian Byzantine Empire fought[4] against Arab or Turkish Muslims, but had lost most of its land in the 12th century.

Key terms

The Holy Land

The Holy Land for Christians means the Land of **Israel**, also known as **Palestine**. But the area is also important[5] for Jews and Muslims. **Jerusalem**, its capital, is the holy city for Jews, Christians and Muslims. Christians have lived in Palestine since the days of Jesus.

Key terms

Crusades[6]

Crusades were **war-pilgrimages** to different places in the Holy Land. The word "crusade" comes from the French word for "cross"[7]. The crusaders[8] wore a red cross on their clothes and banners[9] to show that they were fighting for Christ who had died on the cross.
The aim[10] of the crusades to Palestine was to conquer[11] the holy places (= the places where Jesus lived and died) and take them away from Muslim control. There were altogether seven crusades between 1096 and 1291.

1 to rule *herrschen*
2 throughout the Middle Ages *während des gesamten Mittelalters*
3 capital *Hauptstadt*
4 to fight, fought, fought *kämpfen*
5 important *wichtig*
6 crusade *Kreuzzug*
7 cross *Kreuz*
8 crusader *Kreuzfahrer/in*
9 banner *Fahne*
10 aim *Ziel, Absicht*
11 to conquer *erobern*
12 event *Ereignis*

Task: The First Crusade

Make a timeline of the events[12] which led to the First Crusade.

2.3 Seven wars in two hundred years

S 10 **Crusaders are starting their journey into the Holy Land, book illumination, ca. 1250**

Beginning in November 1095, churchmen[1] travelled around Europe to persuade[2] knights to go on a crusade. In the autumn of 1096, around 60,000 people – knights with their foot soldiers[3], townsmen and peasants[4] – left their homes to go on the 4,000-km journey to Jerusalem. They did not go as simple pilgrims, but as soldiers. This was expensive, so families gave everything they had: horses, as well as gold and silver. They also sold their land so that fathers and sons could go on crusades and be forgiven for the bad things they had done in their lives.

After three hard years of battles[5], hunger and diseases[6], the crusaders reached[7] Jerusalem. They could only enter the city in July 1099 after a siege[8] of five weeks.

After their victory[9], the crusaders founded[10] the **Kingdom of Jerusalem** and other small Christian states in Palestine. The crusaders built strong castles and seemed safe[11] from attack[12]. But in 1187, the Muslims beat[13] the crusaders' army. The crusader families who were still in Palestine could buy their freedom[14] and leave the city. The 15,000 people in crusader families who did not have enough money were sold as slaves[15].

The Pope then called for[16] a new crusade. But in the following wars, the crusaders could not win back Jerusalem. Their last army[17] went back to Europe in 1291.

1 churchman *Geistlicher*
2 to persuade *überzeugen*
3 foot soldier *Fußsoldat/in*
4 peasant *Bauer/Bäuerin*
5 battle *Schlacht*
6 disease *Krankheit*
7 to reach *erreichen*
8 siege *Belagerung*
9 victory *Sieg*
10 to found *gründen*
11 safe *sicher*
12 attack *Angriff*
13 to beat *schlagen*
14 freedom *Freiheit*
15 slave *Sklave/Sklavin*
16 to call for sth. *nach etw. rufen*
17 army *Armee, Heer*

Tasks: Going to Jerusalem

1 Who are the men in the painting (**S 10**)? Are they knights, townsmen or peasants? Explain your answer.

2 Some historians have argued that mostly poorer Europeans went on crusades because they hoped to become rich in the Holy Land. Write down what you think. ***Language Help:*** *to pay for, armour, weapons, costs of travelling.*

S 11 The crusader castle of ▸ *Krak de Chevalier*, today a ▸ World Heritage site[1] in modern Syria

It controlled the only route in the mountains between the coast of the Mediterranean Sea[2] and inland[3] Syria (*Syrien*).
Up to 2,000 soldiers lived in it. They dug[4] through the rocks[5] to make their own water well[6]. They had enough food to survive a five-year siege of Muslim attackers.
To protect[7] the soldiers, the walls were stronger than the walls of European castles. The 13 towers were round, which was unknown in Europe at that time.
In the end, there were only 200 knights left who gave up after a short siege in 1271.

S 12 Extract from Imad ad-Din's chronicle

Imad ad-Din was a Persian historian (1125 –1201). He was present at the battles when Muslim armies won back Palestine and Jerusalem in 1187. He described what happened after they had entered the city.
So the Franks [= Arab name for the European crusaders] looted[8] their own churches. They took everything made of gold and silver: the candelabra[9] and the vases. They also carried off the silk[10] curtains[11]. They broke open and emptied the boxes in the churches and took the treasures[12]. Most of the Franks went to the city of Tyre [= Tyros on the Mediterranean coast]. When Jerusalem was cleaned of the hellish[13] Franks and their dirt, the [non-European] Christians paid their tax[14]. They did not want to leave so they asked to be allowed to stay on in safety[15]. They worked for us with all their energy and did every task with discipline and cheerfulness[16]. They accepted these tasks as if they were gifts.

From: Francesco Gabrieli, Arab historians of the Crusades, New York 2010

Tasks: Christian behaviour through Muslim eyes

1 Read Imad ad-Din's chronicle and list what the crusaders did after they had lost the battle.

2 Imagine you are one of the crusaders who Imad ad-Din described. Give reasons for the things you did. **Language help:** *I took the vases from the church near my house because …*

3 Imagine you are one of the Christians who stayed in Jerusalem and worked for the Muslims. Give your reasons for doing that. **Language help:** *I stayed/paid my tax/worked for the Muslims because …*

4 Explain why Christians did not use the gold and silver from their churches to buy the freedom of the poorer Christians. **Language help:** *They did not buy the poorer Christians' freedom because …*

1 World Heritage site *Weltkulturerbe*
2 Mediterranean Sea *Mittelmeer*
3 inland *Inland, Binnen-*
4 to dig, dug, dug *graben*
5 rock *Felsen*
6 well *Brunnen*
7 to protect *beschützen*
8 to loot *plündern*
9 candelabra *Kandelaber, Kronleuchter*
10 silk *Seide*
11 curtain *Vorhang*
12 treasure *Schatz*
13 hellish *höllisch*
14 tax *Steuer, Abgabe*
15 safety *Sicherheit*
16 cheerfulness *Fröhlichkeit*

Comparing written sources[1]

Authors who lived at the time of the crusades wrote long descriptions about what had happened. Historians call these descriptions ▸**chronicles** (*Chroniken*). Some authors wrote about events which they had seen themselves. Others wrote down what people had told them or what they had learned from other ▸**sources** (letters, reports, etc.).

Sometimes different authors described the same events in the same way, but at other times in a different way. To find out what really happened, historians compare the different chronicles: Which parts of the chronicles are the same? Which are different? Which details are not mentioned?

After that, historians try to find out why the authors described the event. The reason[2] may be that not all authors took part[3] in the events. Maybe they wrote their texts many years later. They could not know all the facts. The authors also had different readers who wanted to learn different things. So they wrote down details which the other authors left out. Sometimes they even exaggerated[4] because they wanted their readers to really understand what they had to say.

What happened when the crusaders entered Jerusalem in 1099?

S 13 Extract from Archbishop William of Tyre's (Wilhelm von Tyrus, 1130–1186) chronicle

William of Tyre grew up in Jerusalem. His family came from Italy or France. He also went to universities in Italy and France. He wrote his chronicle in Latin.

The crusaders went together through the streets with their swords[5] and spears[6] in hand. They killed everybody they met: men, women, and children. There was no mercy[7]. They killed so many in the streets that they had to walk over the dead bodies. ... It would have been sad to see that if these people had not been the enemies[8] of our Lord Jesus Christ.

It was well-fitting[9] that the heathen men and unbelievers ... should pay for their wrong belief[10]. Then the crusaders put on fresh clothes and went to the ▸Church of the Holy Sepulchre[11]. There they prayed and gave thanks ...

From: William of Tyre in: Emily Atwater Babcock and August Charles Krey (eds.), A History of Deeds Done Beyond the Sea, Columbia University Press 1943

S 14 Extract from Ibn al-Athir's (1160–1233) chronicle

Ibn al-Athir was the most important Arab historian in the Middle Ages. He was born in today's Turkey and died in today's Iraq.

In the Al Aqsa Mosque[12] [in Jerusalem], the Franks killed 70,000 people... The Franks took 40 silver candelabra, twenty gold ones, and much more. Muslims from Jerusalem, who had fled[13] to Baghdad [in Iraq], described the sufferings[14] of the Muslims in that holy city of Jerusalem: the men were killed, the women and children were taken prisoner[15], and the homes were looted.

Because they had suffered so[16] much, they were allowed to break the ▸Ramadan fast[17].

From: Ibn al-Athir in: The First Crusade, p. 273

S 15 Al Aqsa mosque

1 written sources *Schriftquellen*
2 reason *Grund*
3 to take part in sth. *an etw. teilnehmen*
4 to exaggerate *übertreiben*
5 sword *Schwert*
6 spear *Speer*
7 mercy *Gnade*
8 enemy *Feind/in*
9 well-fitting *passend, angemessen*
10 belief *Glaube*
11 the Church of the Holy Sepulchre *Grabeskirche*
12 mosque *Moschee*
13 to flee, fled, fled *flüchten, fliehen*
14 suffering (n) *Leiden*
15 to take prisoner *gefangen nehmen*
16 to suffer *leiden*
17 Ramadan fast *Ramadan, islamischer Fastenmonat*

S 16 Extract from Fulcher of Chartres' (1059 – 1127) chronicle

Fulcher, a French churchman, took part in the First Crusade but was not present when the crusaders entered the city of Jerusalem. He stayed in Jerusalem until he died.

Many [Muslims] fled to the roof of the Al Aqsa Mosque and were shot with arrows[1], so that they fell to the ground dead. Almost ten thousand were killed there. Our feet were coloured red to our ankles[2] with the blood of the killed people. Nobody was left alive; no women, no children ...
After the bloodbath was over, the crusaders entered the houses and took whatever they found in them. ... Thus[3] many poor men became rich.
Afterwards, all the churchmen and laymen[4] went to the Church of the Sepulchre of the Lord ... With fitting humility[5], they prayed at the holy places that they had long wanted to visit.

From: Oliver J. Thatcher and Edgar Holmes McNeal (eds.), A Source Book for Medieval History, New York 1905, pp. 513–517

Tasks: Comparing different sources

1 Copy the table and fill it in.

History skills	*Fulcher of Chartres*	*Ibn al-Athir*	*William of Tyre*
Did the author take part in the described events?			no
If not: how long after the events did the author write the text?			
Who is the audience[6] (= who is the text for/who will read the text)?			
Write down in no more than four sentences what the author wrote about the events.			*The crusaders killed every Muslim they met in Jerusalem. They had no mercy. After the bloodbath, they went to church.*
Which sentences give the opinion of the authors?			
Which details are not mentioned by one author, but are mentioned by another?		*Crusaders go to church.*	
If an author does not mention the detail, give a possible reason why.			
Which details may be exaggerated?			

2 Mark in your table the details that are the same in all three accounts. What do you think really happened in Jerusalem? Explain why you think so. ***Language help:*** *The crusaders must/may have really ... because ...*

3 Give reasons for the differences in the accounts. See the Activate your English box on p. 30 and the text on p. 36 for help.

4 Write down the authors' messages to their readers (= what they wanted to tell their readers). ***Language help:*** *Fulcher of Chartres/Ibn al-Athir/William of Tyre (also) wanted to tell his readers that ... Christians/Muslims are ... thieves who ... brutal killers who .../heroes who .../ unbelievers/ good Christians who .... It was right/wrong what happened because ...*

1 arrow *Pfeil*
2 ankle *Knöchel*
3 thus *deswegen, folglich*
4 layman *Laie, Person, die nicht der Kirche angehört*
5 humility *Demut*
6 audience *Publikum*

2.4 East meets west: Effects[1] of the crusades

S 17 **Crusaders are boarding a ship to Palestine, French book illumination, ca. 1350**

The crusades went on for nearly 200 years, but the time when Christians and Muslims actually[2] fought against each other lasted[3] only 24 years. During the long periods of peace[4], Christians and Muslims learned to live and work together.

Europe: New products and ideas from the Muslim world

For the Muslims, the Christians were backward[5] and uncivilized[6]. That is why they had very little interest in Western culture.

The Europeans however, discovered wonderful new things from the Muslims, which they liked very much und had never seen before. Ships, which carried crusaders from Italy to Palestine, brought back silk[7], cotton[8], sugar, exotic fruits like lemons, and spices[9] like pepper.

The Europeans also learned that Muslim Arabs used different symbols for writing numbers: 1, 2, 3, 4 .... They found out that these **Arabic numbers** were much easier to use than the Roman[10] numerals[11] (I, II, III, IV ...), which the Europeans still used.

European languages have borrowed[12] many **words from Arabic**, the language which was spoken in Palestine:

S 18 **Arabic loan words[13] in English and German**

English: *cotton, sofa, mattress, magazine*[14], *arsenal*[15], *admiral, coffee, algebra, lilac, azure*, etc.
German: *Sirup, Tasse, Laute, Gitarre, Aprikose, schachmatt, Satin, Ziffer*, etc.

They show some of the things which where new to Europeans at the time.

1 effect *Auswirkung*
2 actually *tatsächlich*
3 to last *andauern*
4 peace *Frieden*
5 backward *rückständig*
6 uncivilized *unzivilisiert*
7 silk *Seide*
8 cotton *Baumwolle*
9 spice *Gewürz*
10 Roman *römisch*
11 numeral *Zahlensymbol*
12 to borrow *hier: entlehnen*
13 loan word *Lehnwort*
14 magazine *Speicher, Warenlager*
15 arsenal *Arsenal, Waffenlager*

Tasks: East meets west

1 Arabic loan words in German and English. Copy the table and fill in the loan words from above. Can you think of other words from Arabic?

buildings	*Musical instruments*	*Food and drink*	*Fabrics/ cloth?*	*colours*	*...*
					Ziffer
...					

2 In the book illumination **S 17**, you clearly see the coloured banners of the travellers on the ship. Each knight had a banner which showed who he was. Give a possible reason why it was so important for the painter to show the different banners.

Unit revision

Pilgrimages and Crusades

Activate your English
Talking about possible reasons and events

Key Words
Pilgrimage • crusade

Key Person
Urban II

History skills
Comparing written sources

S 19 **Jesus Christ on his way to Jerusalem**
He is followed by his knights. Book illumination, ca. 1310

Revision tasks: Pilgrimages and Crusades

1 Explain what a pilgrimage and a crusade are and who Urban II was. Explain the connection between the pilgrimages to Jerusalem, Urban II, and the first crusade.

2 a Which detail in the book illumination **S 19** tells historians that the knights are crusaders?
b Try to find the painter's message. What did the painter want to tell the readers of the book?
Language help: *The painter wanted to point out/to emphasize that …*

3 Write a definition for the term "crusader".

4 With a partner, write a short interview with a crusader who has just come home from the first crusade. Ask him
- why he went on a crusade,
- about his hopes and dreams,
- what happened in Jerusalem.
- if his dreams had come true,
- if it was right to kill so many Muslim people in Jerusalem because Christians believe it is bad to kill.

3.1 From the Middle Ages[1] …

S1 The medieval[2] view[3] of the solar system[4]

This model shows how the sun and the planets move around the earth, which is at the centre of the solar system.

S2 A medieval drawing of an embryo

Language help: umbilical cord[5], womb[6]

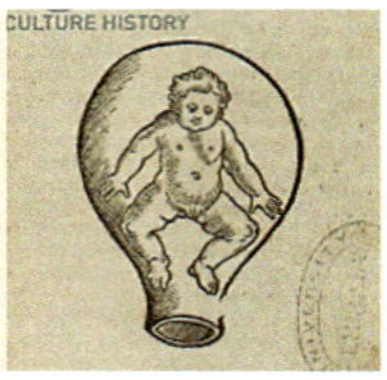

S3 Bonaventura Berlinghieri (ca. 1228–1274), "Madonna and Child with Saints" (ca. 1255)

Paintings in the Middle Ages were hung up in churches and showed scenes and people described in the Bible. The Madonna (Jesus's mother Mary) was painted, for example, so that people could pray[7] to her. Candles[8] were put in front of the painting.
This had an effect on the colours which the artist used. Gold gave the painting a heavenly[9] glow.[10] But gold was the most expensive colour. So the more gold the painter used, the higher the price. Another expensive colour was blue and it was mostly used for the Madonna's clothes.
Artists were not interested in making people look lifelike[11]. So important people were painted larger than others and Mary's son Jesus did not look like a young child, but like a small grown-up.
Artists also did not create natural-looking backgrounds and there were no shadows[12].

1 Middle Ages *Mittelalter*
2 medieval *mittelalterlich*
3 view *Sicht*
4 solar system *Sonnensystem*
5 umbilical cord *Nabelschnur*
6 womb *Mutterleib, Gebärmutter*
7 to pray *beten*
8 candle *Kerze*
9 heavenly *himmlisch*
10 glow (n) *Leuchten*
11 lifelike *naturgetreu*
12 shadow *Schatten*

… to the Early Modern Period

S 4 **Giovanni Bellini (1430–1516), "The Madonna of the Meadow"[1], ca. 1505**

S 5 **A more modern view of the solar system**

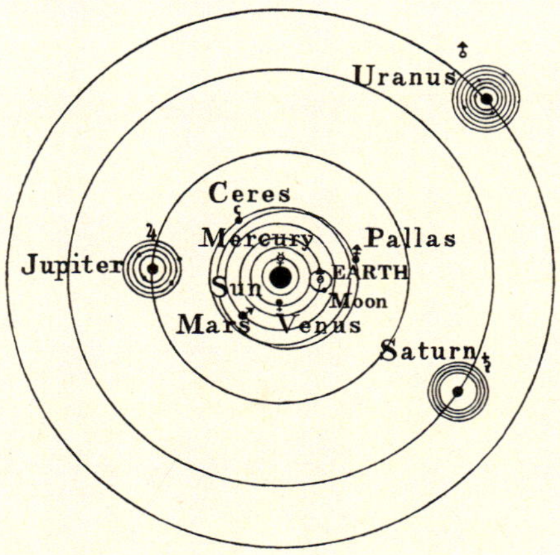

S 6 **▸ Leonardo da Vinci (1452–1519), "Anatomical studies of an embryo"**

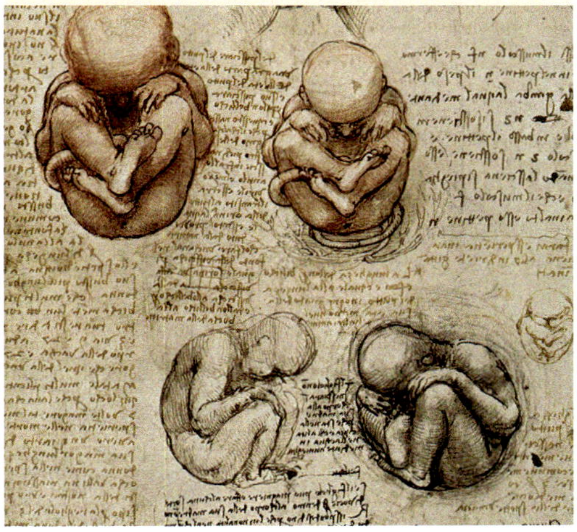

Activate your English

Contrasting[2] ideas and objects

Berlinghieri …, but Bellini …

The Madonna of the Meadow …. Berlinghieri's Madonna however[3] …

Berlinghieri's painting did not … Bellini's painting on the other hand …

In contrast to[4] Berlinghieri's Madonna …

The Madonna of the Meadow … Yet[5] Berlinghieri's Madonna …

Tasks: Comparing and contrasting

1 Compare Bellini's painting with Berlinghieri's. What is different, and what is the same? Use the Activate your English box above for help.

2 Write a caption[6] for **S 5** (A more modern view of the solar system).

1 meadow *Weide*
2 to contrast *kontrastieren, gegenüberstellen*
3 however *jedoch*
4 in contrast to *im Gegensatz zu*
5 yet *dennoch*
6 caption *Bildtext, Beschriftung*

3.2 The birth of a new way of thinking

S7 A book illumination from the end of the 14th century shows a scene at the University of Paris.

In the Middle Ages, the Church ran[1] all schools and universities. The teachers at the schools and the scholars at the universities were all priests[2] or monks[3].

Students had to read about God and heaven[4] in the Bible. Everybody took what the Bible and the Church said to be true (the earth was created in seven days). If people expressed different opinions, the Church would punish[5] them, sometimes by taking their lives.

Students studied mathematics, medicine or astronomy from ancient Greek[6] and Roman[7] books. Most European scholars[8] thought that the ancient[9] authors had answered all the questions about the world. Few doubted[10] what they read in the books. Nobody checked[11] whether the authors were right.

But in the 15th century this changed. Scholars wondered if what the Bible or the ancient authors said was really correct. More and more scholars became curious as to whether the world was like the Church taught it was. They began to ask critical questions and did not accept[12] the answers of the Church. They observed[13] and studied nature themselves; they developed[14] their own theories and predictions[15], experimented, and even dared[16] to publish[17] their findings. The scholars now had evidence[18] that proved[19] their findings and that could be tested by others. They developed what we now call the **scientific[20] method**.

Scholars and students communicated with each other over long distances. They also travelled all across Europe to the great medieval universities, from Bologna (Italy) to Paris, to Oxford and Salamanca (Spain). Because of this, the new ideas spread[21].

Their critical and curious attitude was the basis for the great (scientific) discoveries of the following centuries. These discoveries helped to make the European countries politically, economically and militarily strong.

1 to run sth. *etw. führen*
2 priest *Priester*
3 monk *Mönch*
4 heaven *(biblischer) Himmel*
5 to punish *bestrafen*
6 Greek *griechisch*
7 Roman *römisch*
8 scholar *Gelehrte/r*
9 ancient *antik, klassisch*
10 to doubt sth. *etw. an-/bezweifeln*
11 to check sth. *etw. überprüfen*
12 to accept *hinnehmen, akzeptieren*
13 to observe *beobachten*
14 to develop *entwickeln*
15 prediction *Vorhersage*
16 to dare sth. *etw. wagen*
17 to publish *veröffentlichen*
18 evidence (no pl.!) *Beweis(e)*
19 to prove *beweisen*
20 scientific *wissenschaftlich*
21 to spread *sich ausbreiten*
22 Latin *Latein*
23 Dutch *holländisch*
24 Belgium *Belgien*
25 necessary *notwendig*
26 to put sth. aside *etw. beiseitelegen*
27 prejudice *Vorurteil*
28 science *Wissenschaft*
29 decree *Dekret, Urteil*

S8 An extract from a letter in Latin[22] from the Dutch[23] scholar Agricola (1444–1485) to his friend Jacob Barbirianus in 1484

At that time Agricola lived in Heidelberg and his younger friend in Antwerp (*Antwerpen*), in today's Belgium[24]. In his letter he tries to help his friend with his studies.

... But it is necessary[25] that you should put aside[26] the teaching which has been given to us as boys at school. Give up all that you have learned in this field, together with the prejudices[27] that go along with it ... Science[28] needs evidence and not official decrees[29] which tell you what to teach and believe.

From: Merrick Whitcomb, A Literary Sourcebook of the German Renaissance, 1900, pp. 12–23

Tasks: A new way of thinking

1 **a** Sum up what Agricola writes. Use your own words as much as possible. ***Language help:*** *to claim, to demand.*

b Explain what is new about his way of thinking. Language help: It was normal in the 15th century that, ... but Agricola thought ...

2 **a** Who's who in the book illumination? (**S7**)

b Compare it to your classroom today. Use the Activate your English box on p. 41 for help.

Analysing letters as historical sources[1]

The study of history begins with ▸ **sources**. Historians use different sources to get information about the past: books, magazines, newspapers, government[2] documents, posters, laws[3], paintings and other pictures, buildings and objects, etc. Some of these were made for a large audience[4] and published.
Letters can also be used to find out about the past. There are **different types of letters**:
- Official letters (e.g. a king writes to his ministers)
- Private letters (e.g. a person writes to his/her friend)

Most letters have not survived because the recipients[6] did not keep them. Sometimes letters of famous people may be collected and published.

S9 **Extract[7] from a letter from Leonardo Da Vinci to the Duke[8] of Milan (*Mailand, Italien*), 1482**

In this letter, Leonardo applied[9] for a job at the Duke's court. He began to work as his military engineer[10] in the same year and stayed in Milan for the next seventeen years. During that time he got the chance to experiment[11] with painting, sculpture, architecture, as well as with the design of weapons[12] and machinery.

I can construct bridges which are very light and can be easily moved.
I can also make a kind of cannon which is light and easy to transport.
And I know how to construct many engines[13] either for attack or defense at sea.
In times of peace, I believe that I can construct public and private buildings.
Also in painting, I can do as much as anyone else, whoever he may be.
I could also make for you the bronze statue of your father on a horse which you have planned ... this will make your family even more famous.

From: Robert John Goldwater, Marco Treves (ed) Artists on Art, London 1947, p. 55

History skills	Activate your English
Who wrote the letter? When and where was the letter written?	*The source is an extract from a letter. It was written by ... in [place] in [year].*
What do we know about the author? What was his/her nationality? Was the author a minister, army general, scientist, artist, ...? Where did the author live and/or work, ...?	*The author was a/an (German, Italian, Dutch, English) ...* *He lived/worked in ...*
Who was the letter addressed to? A friend, family members, a member of the government? What is known about this person?	*The letter was written to ..., who was .../ who lives .../works as ...*
Why was the letter written? What was the intention[14] of the author?	*... wrote the letter to inform about an event/to give advice[15] / to persuade[16] / to demand ...* *The author's intention was to ...*
What did the author write?	*In his/her letter ... first described/warned ...* *Then ... explained/criticized[17] ...* *The writer also pointed out that ...* *At the end, he/she claimed that ...*

Tasks: Applying for a job

1 Which skills does Leonardo mention[18] first, and which at the end? ***Language help:*** *First he mentions his ability[19] to ... At the end ...*

2 Give possible reasons for this order.

1 source *Quelle*
2 government *Regierung*
3 law *Gesetz*
4 audience *Publikum*
5 king *König*
6 recipient *Empfänger/in*
7 extract *Auszug*
8 Duke *Herzog*
9 to apply for sth. *sich um etw. bewerben*
10 engineer *Ingenieur/in*
11 to experiment *experimentieren*
12 weapon *Waffe*
13 engine *Maschine*
14 intention *Absicht*
15 to give sb. advice *jmdm. einen Rat erteilen*
16 to persuade *überzeugen*
17 to criticize *kritisieren*
18 to mention *erwähnen*
19 ability *Fähigkeit*

3.3 A new way of painting

S 10 **Carlo Crivelli (ca. 1435 – ca. 1495), "Annunciation[1] with St. Emidius", 1486**

The painting was an altarpiece[2] for a church in Ascoli, Italy. It shows the Archangel Gabriel, who is telling Mary that she will be the mother of Jesus, God's son. The town of Ascoli can still be recognized today in the model which Emidius, the patron saint of Ascoli, is carrying in his hands.

Renaissance art

▸ **Leonardo da Vinci** painted during the period known by art historians as the ▸ **Renaissance** (a French word meaning rebirth[3]), which began in Italy in the 14th century. During that time, Italian scholars and artists began to look again at what the ancient Greek and Roman artists, sculptors, architects, and writers had created[4]. Renaissance artists decided that these works were superior[5] to those produced in the Middle Ages. Painters now wanted to create **realistic paintings** like those produced by the **ancient Greeks and Romans**.

Making paintings more lifelike

Slowly, painters learned that people in the foreground had to be painted bigger than those in the middle ground and background. Artists also found out that buildings and objects had to be painted smaller and smaller the further away they were so as to give the illusion of distance. As a result, their paintings seem to be three-dimensional[6].

Artists' tricks

Artists used "tricks" to give depth[7] to their works. They showed different groups of people, animals, buildings and objects from very near to far away in a realistic and detailed[8] way, even in the background of the painting. They also included[9] things like tiled[10] floor, with the tiles getting smaller towards[11] the back of the room. They always had many diagonal lines in their paintings too. These "met" in the distance, as they do if you look down a road.

People were amazed[12] when they saw this modern art because they had never seen anything so realistic and beautiful before.

1 annunciation *Verkündigung*
2 altarpiece *Altarbild*
3 rebirth *Wiedergeburt*
4 to create *(er)schaffen*
5 superior (adj.) to sth. *besser als etw.*
6 three-dimensional *dreidimensional, räumlich*
7 depth *Tiefe*
8 detailed *detailliert, genau*
9 to include sth. *etw. einschließen, einfügen*
10 tiled *gekachelt, gefliest*
11 towards *in Richtung, entgegen*
12 amazed *überrascht, verblüfft*

Task: Analysing Renaissance paintings

Identify a) the different groups of people/animals/buildings in the foreground, middle ground and background; b) diagonal lines in **S 10**.

3.4 Leonardo da Vinci

Leonardo – a genius?

One of the most famous artists, both in his own time and today, was ▸ **Leonardo da Vinci.** He painted one of the best-known paintings in the world: the Mona Lisa. Thousands visit the Louvre museum in Paris each day to see it. Leonardo, however, was more than a master painter. He was interested in finding out something about everything. His curiosity[1] was unlimited[2]. Leonardo spent a lot of time studying the body of humans[3] and animals and how they worked. He wanted to know exactly how muscles and bodies moved so he dissected[4] at least 30 human corpses[5]. Then he made detailed notes and illustrations in his many notebooks, which showed that he was not only a great artist, but also a brilliant scientist. Although he wanted to publish his notes he never did. So he left behind almost 6,000 pages of unpublished drawings, not only of his observations[6], but also of experiments and plans: plans for submarines, tanks, helicopters, bicycles, and telescopes. His helicopter would not have flown, but many of his other inventions[7] would have worked.

S 11 Examples of notes and illustrations in Leonardo da Vinci's notebooks

The muscles of an arm and a mobile bridge for the military

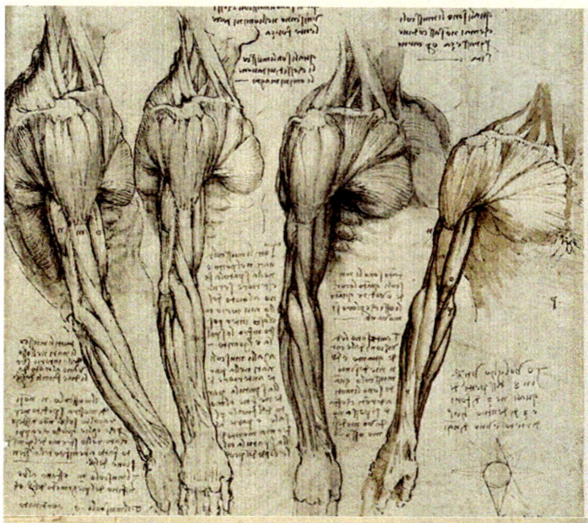

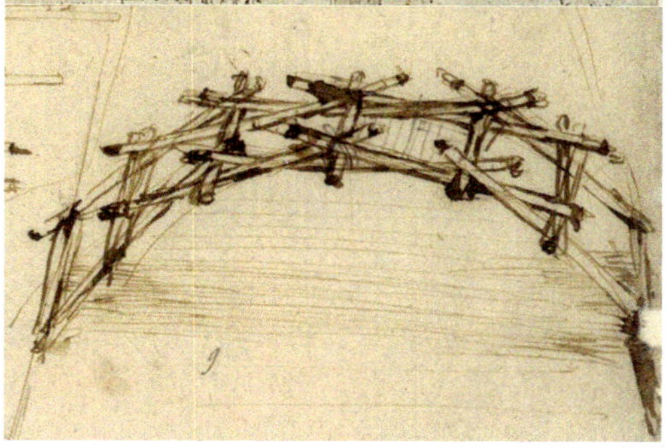

Leonardo's patrons

In the Renaissance, some artists did not create a work of art first and then tried to find a buyer for it. They had patrons[8]. Those were people who paid an artist to work for him or her. They told the artist exactly what they wanted: a Madonna and child, a portrait of a husband's beautiful wife, or a statue of somebody's father.

Leonardo worked for different people at different times. At first he worked for the House of Medici. They were the rulers of Florence and the richest family in Italy (and perhaps in Europe), who spent a lot of money on churches and hospitals, as well as on art. Then, after several[9] years, Leonardo decided to move to Milan (*Mailand*) to work for the Duke of Milan. After that, he worked as a military engineer for an Italian army commander. Finally, at the end of his life, Leonardo da Vinci was an architect, engineer and painter for the French King Francis I (1494–1547).

Tasks: The Life of Leonardo da Vinci

1 Find out more about da Vinci's life:
- where and when he was born/where and when he died
- family
- training
- job
- titles of his paintings.

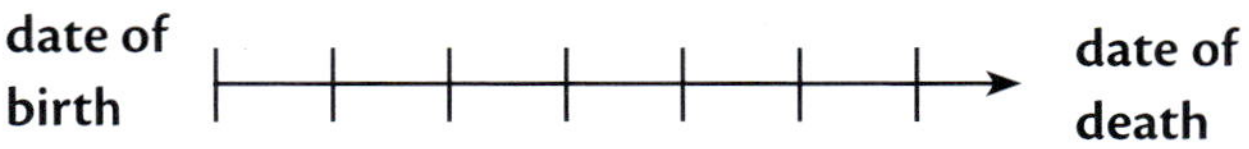

2 Make a timeline of his life.

3 Make a poster. Include a self-portrait of da Vinci on it.

1 curiosity *Neugier, Wissbegier*
2 unlimited *grenzenlos, unbegrenzt*
3 human (n) *Mensch*
4 to dissect *sezieren*
5 human corpse *menschlicher Körper, Leiche*
6 observation *Beobachtung*
7 invention *Erfindung*
8 patron *Förderer*
9 several *mehrere*

3.5 Does the earth move around the sun?

S 12 This computer image shows a reconstruction of what Copernicus may have looked like.

In 2012 scientists identified[1] a skull, which they found in a Frombork church, as Copernicus's skull.

Copernicus's theory

During the Middle Ages, most scholars believed that the earth was the centre of the universe and that the moon, the sun, and the planets all moved in circles around it. Everybody could see that. Did the sun not rise in the morning and set in the evening?

The idea came from ancient Greek and Roman astronomers. In addition, the Church taught that the earth was a special place and that God had put it at the centre of the universe. This view of the solar system was called the ▸ **geocentric theory.**

▸ **Nicolaus Copernicus** felt that this theory was incorrect. In his free time, he observed the sky. He came to think that every planet, including the earth, moved around the sun (▸ **heliocentric theory**). He did not publish the results of his observations for a long time. Historians do not know if he feared the criticism[2] of other astronomers or of the church. He only allowed[3] his theories to be printed[4] at the end of his life.

Galileo Galilei's discoveries[5]

As a young man, ▸ **Galileo Galilei** learned that a Dutch[6] lens[7] maker had built an instrument that could make far away objects look bigger and closer. This was called a telescope. Galileo built his own much better telescope and used it to study the sky in 1609.

Then, in 1610, he published a small 24-page book called "Starry Messenger" (*Sidereus Nuncius*), which described his astonishing[8] observations: the moon, for example, had mountains and the planet Jupiter had four moons.

His work on astronomy made him famous and he was appointed[9] court[10] mathematician in Florence. Galileo's observations also clearly supported[11] the theories of Copernicus.

Conflict with the Church

Galileo's discoveries frightened Church leaders because they disagreed[12] with what the Church taught. If people believed that the Church could be wrong about this, they could ask critical questions about other Church teachings as well.

In 1616, the Catholic Church warned Galileo not to defend[13] the ideas of Copernicus. However, in 1632, he published another book. It clearly showed that Galileo supported the Copernican theory.

A year later, the Catholic Church put Galileo on trial[14] for his "crimes"[15]. Because he feared for his life, he publicly[16] took back what he had written. Galileo was never again a free man. He lived under house arrest until his death at his villa near Florence. However, his books and ideas still spread all over Europe.

In 1992, Pope John Paul II admitted[17] that Galileo had been right.

It took 360 years until the Church officially accepted Galileo's theories.

1 to identify *identifizieren*
2 criticism *Kritik*
3 to allow *erlauben*
4 to print *drucken*
5 discovery *Entdeckung*
6 Dutch (adj.) *holländisch*
7 lens *Linse*
8 astonishing *erstaunlich*
9 to appoint *ernennen*
10 court *Hof*
11 to support *unterstützen*
12 to disagree *nicht einverstanden sein*
13 to defend *verteidigen*
14 to put sb. on trial (for sth.) *jmdn. (wegen etw.) vor Gericht stellen*
15 crime *Verbrechen*
16 publicly (adv.) *öffentlich*
17 to admit *zugeben*

S 13 **Unknown artist, portrait of Galileo Galilei with a telescope in his hand, 1636**

Key terms

Heretic
In medieval times the Church called somebody a "heretic" who had ideas that were different or the opposite[8] from what the Church said.
One of the punishments[9] was burning at the stake[10].

S 14 **Galileo Galilei, extract from a letter to the Grand Duchess Christina of Tuscany, 1615**

Some years ago ... I discovered[1] in the heavens many things that had not been seen before our own age.
Because these things were so new, quite a number of professors began to make trouble for me ... Because they liked their own opinions[2] better than the truth[3], they stated that the new things were not true.

But if they had cared to look for themselves, their own senses would have demonstrated that the new things existed. They knew that I believed that the sun does not move in the centre of our solar system, but rather that the earth moves around the sun.
To destroy[4] me, they first tried to spread the opinion that such statements are in conflict with the Bible and are consequently[5] damnable[6]. They tried to make this opinion seem new and to belong to me alone. They pretended[7] not to know that its author ... was Nicholas Copernicus ...
When his book was printed, it was accepted by the Holy Church, and it has been read and studied by everyone. Nobody protested. Yet now that necessary proofs have shown his theories to be well grounded, they call him a heretic. They say that the Bible cannot be wrong.

From: Paul Halsall, Modern History Sourcebook, http://www.fordham.edu/halsall/mod/galileo-tuscany.asp, 1997

Tasks: Defending Galileo Galilei

1 Sum up what Galileo wrote about how Copernicus and he were criticized. Use your own words as much as possible. The following words will help you: to explain, to claim, to give reasons why, to argue, to defend.
Language help: *In his letter, Galileo explains ... He claims that ... He defends himself and says ...*

2 **a** Imagine you were the one who had to write the arguments against Galileo in the trial. Write down the arguments.
b How does Galileo defend[11] himself? Act out the scene in class.

Tasks: The Life of Copernicus and Galileo

1 Find out more about Copernicus's/Galileo's life:
- where and when he was born/where and when he died,
- his family,
- the school/university he went to,
- his job,
- titles of his books and when were they published,
- when did Pope John Paul II declare that Galileo had been right?

2 Make a timeline of his life.

3 Make a poster about his life.

1 to discover sth. *etw. entdecken*
2 opinion *Meinung, Überzeugung*
3 truth *Wahrheit*
4 to destroy sth. *etw. zerstören*
5 consequently *folglich*
6 damnable *verdammenswert*
7 to pretend *vorgeben, so tun als ob*
8 opposite (n) *Gegenteil*
9 punishment *Bestrafung*
10 (to) burn at the stake *auf dem Scheiterhaufen brennen*
11 to defend *verteidigen*

3.6 Don't believe everything you read – Andreas Vesalius and dissection[1]

S 15 From the title page of ▸ Vesalius's book *De humani corporis fabrica* (On the Structure of the Human Body), 1543

Professor Vesalius (on the left) is giving a lesson and is dissecting a corpse in front of his students at Padua University.

Medieval medicine

Till 1500, the most important book about medicine was a book written by ▸ **Claudius Galen**, a Greek doctor in the second century AD[2]. To find out how the human body worked, he dissected the corpses of monkeys and pigs. For religious reasons however, he was not allowed to dissect human corpses[3]. Galen thought that the structure of the human body was much the same.

Medical students in the Middle Ages read his works to learn about human bodies, but they did not study human bodies themselves or dissect them.

Andreas Vesalius

In the 16th century however, ▸ **Andreas Vesalius** proved that Galen had been wrong in many ways. He dissected hundreds of human corpses himself. As a student, he even stole parts of the body of an executed[4] criminal to use it for his studies.

Some years later, hundreds came to watch his lectures at Padua University. He also encouraged[5] his students to examine the human body for themselves.

A complete map of the human body

Vesalius's discoveries were first published in his book "On the Structure of the Human Body" (*De humani corporis fabrica*) in 1543. Its accurate[6] illustrations were made by the best artists in Italy and for the first time gave a complete map of the human body. It showed, for example, how nerves and muscles are connected.

Since his book was printed after the invention of the **printing press** (see p. 63), Vesalius's ideas spread quickly throughout Europe[7].

However, the study of the human body did not change overnight. Many doctors opposed[8] Vesalius, partly because he was young and partly because he refused[9] some of Galen's ideas.

1 dissection *Sezieren, innere Leichenschau*
2 AD (= anno Domini) *nach Christus*
3 human corpse *menschlicher Körper, Leiche*
4 to execute *hinrichten*
5 to encourage *ermutigen*
6 accurate *genau, exakt*
7 throughout Europe *in ganz Europa*
8 to oppose sb./sth. *sich jdm./etw. entgegenstellen*
9 to refuse sth. *etw. ablehnen*

Tasks: The life of Andreas Vesalius

1 Find out more about Vesalius:
- where and when he was born/where and when he died,
- family,
- school/university,
- job,
- titles of his books.

2 Make a timeline of his life.

3 Make a poster about his life.

Unit revision

A New Age of Art and Learning

Key personalities

Leonardo da Vinci • Nicolaus Copernicus • Galileo Galilei • Andreas Vesalius

History skills

Analysing letters • making timelines • presenting biographies

Key terms

Scientific method • geocentric and helio-centric theory • Renaissance art • heretic

Activate your English

Contrasting ideas and objects

Revision tasks: A New Age of Art and Learning

1 Choose one of the letters in this unit and write an analysis (see p. 43 for help)

2 Explain how Bellini tried to make the Madonna, her child and the world around them look lifelike in his painting (p. 41).

3 a Finish what Galileo and Vesalius are saying in the cartoons above.
  b Give possible reasons why this could be very dangerous for the person who said this.

4 Describe the difference between how students learn in **S 7** on p. 42 and **S 15** on p. 48.

5 a Describe the cartoon. (What does Galileo show the churchman? What would the churchman like to do?)
  b Discuss whether churchmen might have really thought in the same way as the churchman in the cartoon. Give reasons why.

GALILEO DESCRIBES HIS DISCOVERIES TO THE CHURCH

The Age[1] of Discovery[2]

4.1 No voyages[3] without maps

S 1

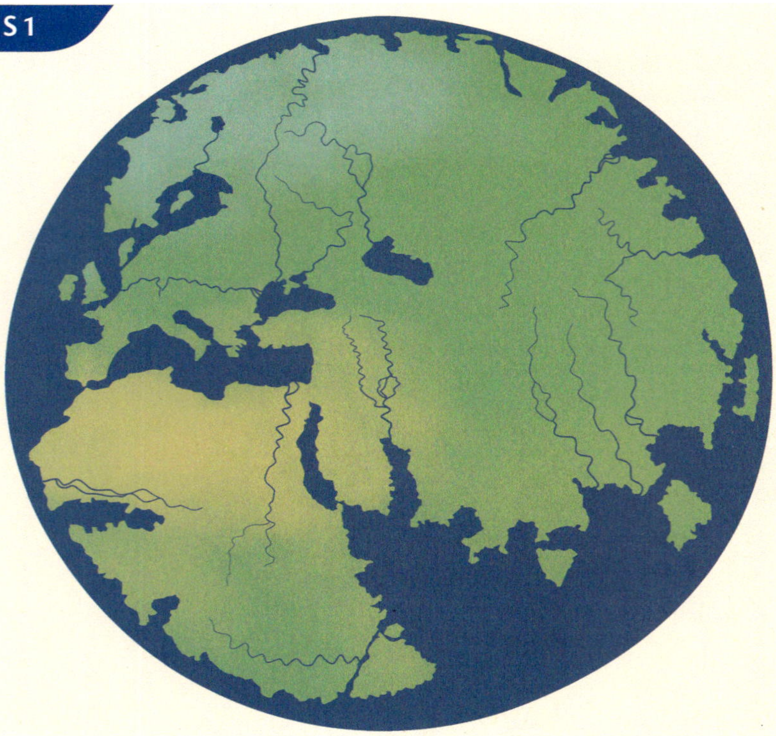

A modern drawing[5] of the original map by Fra Mauro from around 1450 (fourteen fifty), about 2 metres in diameter[6]

Fra Mauro was a monk[7] and map maker[8] in Venice (*Venedig*), Italy. The Portuguese King Alfonso V (the fifth) asked him to make a map of the world.

When seamen and merchants[9] went on voyages by sea at the beginning of the 15th century they had maps, but their maps did not show the real world. They knew that the earth was a sphere[10], but they did not know how big the sphere was, how big the continents and oceans were, or where exactly the continents were on this sphere.

The Italian doctor and map maker ▸ Paolo Toscanelli (1397 – 1482 = thirteen ninety-seven to fourteen eighty-two) tried to find out how big the Atlantic Ocean was and how long it would take to cross it. He began to read all the texts about voyages to East Asia and Africa. He asked merchants and seamen who came to Italy from all different parts of the world. Then he made a completely new type of map. It showed Asia directly across from Portugal (see p. 51). Toscanelli also wrote to King Alfonso that the Atlantic Ocean was not as large as they had thought. Ships could sail west across the Atlantic Ocean to reach[11] India. But King Alfonso did not believe him. The person who did believe Toscanelli and wanted to prove[12] him right was ▸ Christopher Columbus (1451 – 1506 = fifteen o six), a sea captain from Genoa (*Genua*) in Italy. But who would pay for this voyage?

Tasks: Map makers and voyages

1 **a** Tell your partner which continents, rivers and seas you recognize[13] in Fra Mauro's map (**S 1**).
b Which continents are not on the map?

2 Start a list of all the countries/continents and their people in this unit.

Country or continent	***people***
Italy	*Italian*
Europe	...

1 age *(Zeit-)Alter*
2 Age of Discovery *Zeitalter der Entdeckungen*
3 voyage *lange (See-)Reise*
5 drawing *Zeichnung*
6 diameter *Durchmesser*
7 monk *Mönch*
8 map maker *Kartenzeichner (Kartograph)*
9 merchant *Kaufmann*
10 sphere *hier: Kugel*
11 to reach *erreichen*
12 to prove *beweisen*
13 to recognize *wiedererkennen*

Analysing diagrams and historical maps

S2 A modern version of Toscanelli's map. The original map is from 1474.

It shows the Atlantic Ocean and where Toscanelli believed Northern China, Southern China and Japan were.

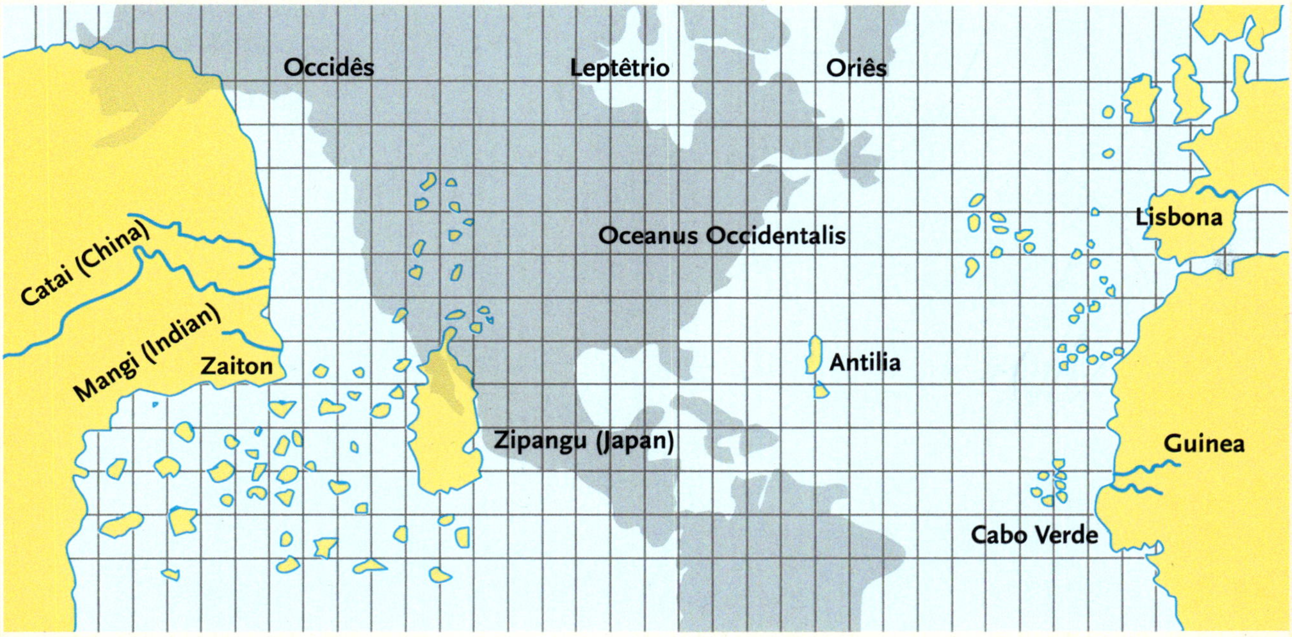

Key[1]: yellow = land on Toscanelli's map
grey = the Americas on modern maps

Key terms

America: South or North America
the Americas: North, Central, South America and the West Indies

History skills

Title: What is the title of the map/diagram? What area is shown on the map? What does the map tell us about the time when it was made?

Key: What information is given in the key? What do the different colours/symbols stand for?

Content: What information (about areas, events[2], people, changes of borders[3] ...) does the map/diagram give?

Activate your English

The map/diagram is called ...
It shows ... (area)
It tells us that in ... (year) people thought that ...

The key shows ...
The different colours/symbols stand for[4] ...
For example, green is for/stands for ...

The map/diagram shows/mentions[5] ... (the different.../where.../how.../...)

1 key *hier: Legende, Bilderklärung*
2 event *Ereignis*
3 border *Grenze*
4 to stand for sth. *für etw. stehen, bedeuten*
5 to mention *erwähnen, nennen*

4.2 Europeans found the way to *India*

S3 Voyages of discovery till 1522

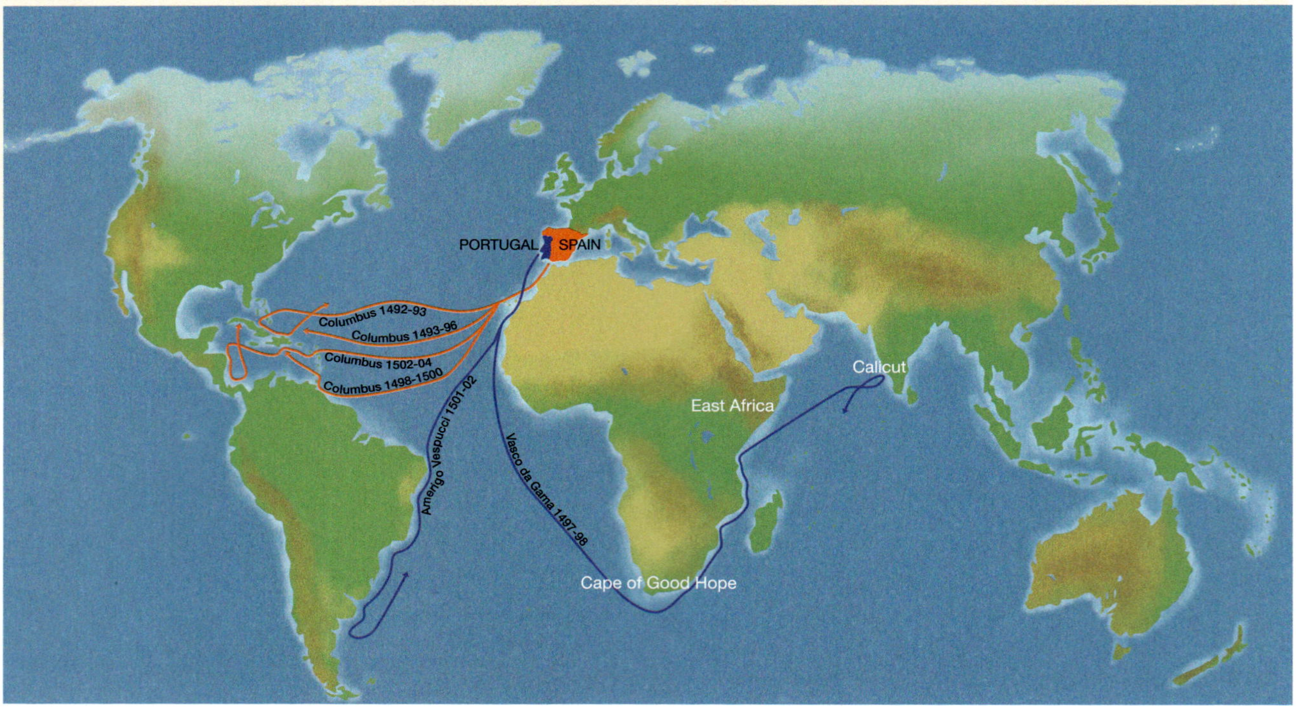

The Portuguese sailed[1] east around Africa to reach India

In the 14th and 15th century, spices[2] like pepper from India and China reached Europe from the East after long and dangerous voyages. Because spices had become very expensive, European merchants hoped for a faster sea trade route[3] to India. Spices would then be much cheaper. Around 1450, the Portuguese ▸ **Prince Henry** (1394 – 1460) paid sea captains and map makers to explore[4] the African coast. Was it possible to sail around Africa to reach India? But many seamen were afraid of that voyage. Would it be too hot in the south? Were monsters living there? However, year after year new Portuguese ships sailed south along the African coast till ▸ **Bartolomeo Diaz** (1450 – 1500) reached the Cape of Good Hope[5] in South Africa in 1486. ▸ **Vasco da Gama** (1469 – 1524) then landed in East Africa and in the Indian city of Calicut[6] in 1498.

Sailing west – a faster way to India?

The Spanish Queen Isabella and her husband Ferdinand II supported[7] and paid **Christopher Columbus**. They thought it was the duty[8] of all Christians[9] to bring their religion to the people in India. Columbus argued[11] that Toscanelli was right and he could reach India if he sailed westward and crossed the Atlantic Ocean west of Spain. The new type of ship with its compass and better sails would make it possible. However[12], others argued that no one knew what was on the other side of the ocean or how far away India really was from Europe. The voyage might take too long and the crew could die of hunger. Only some years later did the king and queen give Columbus the money for the voyage.
Of course, Columbus never imagined[13] that a whole continent lay between Europe and India!

1 to sail *segeln*
2 spice *Gewürz*
3 trade route *Handelsweg*
4 to explore *erforschen*
5 Cape of Good Hope *Kap der Guten Hoffnung*
6 Calicut *Kalkutta, heute: Kozhikode in Südindien*
7 to support *unterstützen*
8 duty *Pflicht*
9 Christian (n, v) *christlich, Christ*
11 to argue *argumentieren*
12 however *jedoch*
13 to imagine sth. *sich etw. vorstellen*

S 4 Columbus's first experience[1] meeting the Native[2] Americans, as written by Columbus in the ship's logbook:

I think that the people are clever. They would be good servants[3] and would very easily become Christians, as they appear to have no religion. They are quick learners [...] I will take six of them back to Spain [...] so that they may learn our language.

From: Bartolomé de las Casas, Journal of the First Voyage, ca. 1516

S 5 Christopher Columbus painted by Sebastiano del Piombo in 1519, thirteen years after Columbus's death

4.3 A new continent?

On August 3, 1492, Columbus left Spain with three ships which were between 15 and 36 metres long. The 87 men on the ship were mostly prisoners[4], because Columbus had not found enough volunteers[5] for the voyage. In September, they reached the Canary Islands[6] and on October 12, 1492, they discovered an island in the Bahamas. In the name of the Spanish kings, Columbus took possession[7] of the island and called it San Salvador. A month later they arrived at the islands which are called Cuba and Hispaniola today. Columbus believed that he had landed on islands near India, so he incorrectly called the people who he met on the islands "**Indians**" and the islands the ▸ "**West Indies**".
During his life, Columbus made three more voyages to the so-called[8] ▸ **New World**, but he never found a route to bring spices from India to Europe. Columbus still believed that he had found India when he died in 1506.
On later voyages, other seamen realized that they had found a *new* continent. One of them was ▸ **Amerigo Vespucci** (ca. 1454 – 1512) who explored the Brazilian coast. When a German map maker drew a map of this voyage in 1507, he gave this new continent Vespucci's first name: **America**.

1 experience *Erfahung, Erlebnis*
2 native (n, adj.) *Einheimische/r, einheimisch*
3 servant *Diener/in*
4 prisoner *Gefangene/r*
5 volunteer *Freiwillige/r*
6 Canary Islands *Kanarische Inseln*
7 to take possession of *in Besitz nehmen*
8 so-called *sogenannt*

Key term

Native Americans are the group of people who lived in the Americas before the Europeans arrived. They do not like to be called 'Indians'.

Tasks: Portuguese and Spanish voyages of discovery

1 Make a timeline of the *Portuguese and Spanish voyages of discovery*.
Don't forget to put in the dates. Use the prepositions *on*, *around* or *in* before the date.

What happened?	*Date*
Portuguese ships explored the African coast	*around 1450*
Vasco da Gama reached East Africa and the Indian city of Calicut	?

Then ask your partner: What happened around …? When did … reach …?

2 Who did what?
a The Portuguese sent ships along the African coast to find the sea route to India.
b Columbus argued that the … doctor of medicine Toscanelli was right.
c The … sent Columbus west.
d Columbus thought when he landed on an island in the Bahamas that he was in … so he called the people on the island …
e A … mapmaker called the new continent America.

3 Use the History skills on p. 51 to analyse maps **S 2** and **3**.

4 Write down what Columbus may have told people about his life.

When I was young I dreamt of finding a way to India …

5 Discuss what surprises you about Columbus's plans and ideas about Native Americans (**S 4**).

4.4 The Spanish conquered[1] and destroyed the Aztec[2] and Inca[3] Empires[4]

S6 The page from the Florentine Codex[5] shows Cortés's men leaving their ships

Between 1540 and 1585 ▸ Bernardino de Sahagún, a Spanish priest, asked the Aztecs to write about their lives before the Spanish conquered Central America. The book has texts in the Aztec language, in Spanish and in Latin. It also has 1,800 drawings. It is called the Florentine Codex because it is kept in a library in Florence (*Florenz*), Italy. The Codex has been the most important source of information about Aztec life before 1519.

1 to conquer *erobern*
2 Aztec *Azteken, mittelamerikanische Kultur und Bevölkerung vom 14.-16. Jh. im Bereich des heutigen Mexiko*
3 Inca *Inka, südamerikanische Stadtkultur und Bevölkerung vom 13.-16. Jh.*
4 empire *Reich, Imperium*
5 codex *Kodex, alte Buchform*
6 capital *hier: Hauptstadt*
7 powerful *mächtig*
8 army *Armee*
9 wealthy *wohlhabend*
10 bows and arrows *Pfeil und Bogen*
11 to treat sb. *jmd. behandeln*
12 to sacrifice *opfern*
13 as a result *daher, folglich*
14 to drive (drove, driven) off *vertreiben*

S7 Inca and Aztec Empires before the arrival of the Spanish in 1519

Cortés conquered the Aztec empire

In 1519 the Spanish captain and soldier ▸ **Hernán Cortés** (1485 – 1547) sailed from Cuba to Mexico with around 600 men, 16 horses and 4 cannons to look for the "land of gold and silver". He wanted to conquer this land for the Spanish kings and use it to become rich himself.
Cortés and his men arrived in Mexico and began travelling towards ▸ **Tenochtitlán**, the capital[6] of the wealthy ▸ **Aztec Empire** in the highlands of Mexico. At that time, the king, **Moctezuma II** (1465 – 1520), had a powerful[7] army[8] and was very wealthy[9] because he had conquered other cities. However, the Aztecs did not have horses or guns and fought only with bows and arrows[10].

Many of the people in the cities which the Aztecs had conquered were unhappy about the way the Aztecs treated[11] them. They had to pay them in gold and food. The Aztecs were also brutal, and often sacrificed[12] the conquered people to their gods. As a result[13], many of these cities fought against the Aztecs with Cortés and his men.
At first the Aztecs welcomed the Spanish. They thought that the Spanish were the gods which old legends had promised would come. When at last, they tried to drive off[14] the Spanish, it was too late. After two years, the small Spanish army had conquered the Aztec Empire.

Tenochtitlán

Tenochtitlán, the Aztec capital, was a city which was built on an island in the middle of a shallow[1] lake. It was connected to the mainland[2] by three roads which were built on dams. Around 200,000 people lived there. The Spanish described it as extremely beautiful with clean, straight and wide streets. The smaller streets were half on land, half canals, where the people paddled their canoes. Fresh water was brought to the island by stone aqueducts[3]. The Great Temple for the god of war and for rain was in the centre. Nearby were palaces with their gardens, a big marketplace, and schools. Most of the people in the city were farmers who produced vegetables on small islands in the lake.

S 8 **Florentine Codex**

S 9 **Cortés's map of Tenochtitlán of 1524**

The two largest temples in Tenochtitlán were pyramids with flat tops, where the priests cut out the hearts of prisoners of war[4] – men, women and children. The Aztecs believed that without human[5] blood, the sun would not rise[6] the next day and the world would end. Cortés estimated[7] that 20,000 people had already been killed for the gods that year when he arrived in the city in November 1519. This seemed horrible to the Christian Spanish people.

Tasks: Spanish conquerors

1 Describe the drawing in **S 6**. Identify[8] the animals the Spanish brought with them. Give possible reasons why they brought them.

2 Write a caption[9] for **S 8**.

3 Describe the map of Tenochtitlán (**S 9**). Begin like this: The map shows … at the time when … We can also see … (s. History skills *Analysing diagrams and historical maps*, p. 51).
Language help: mainland – *Festland*; aqueduct – *Aquädukt*; dam – *Damm*

1 shallow *flach*
2 mainland *Festland*
3 aqueduct *Aquäduct, Wasserleitung*
4 prisoner of war *Kriegsgefangene/r*
5 human (adj.) *menschlich*
6 to rise (rose, risen) *aufgehen, steigen*
7 to estimate *schätzen*
8 to identify *hier: bestimmen, ermitteln*
9 caption *Bildtext, Beschriftung*

S 10/11 **Florentine codex: becoming ill and dying of ▸ smallpox**

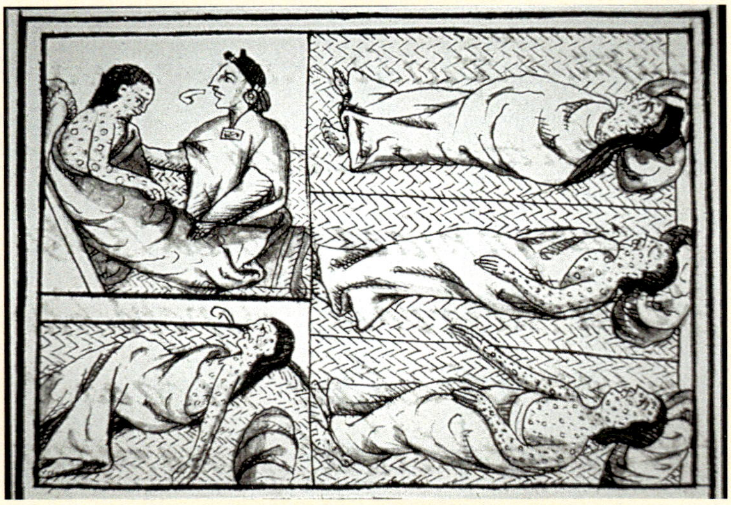

"An epidemic[1] broke out, a sickness of pustules[2]. It began in Tepeilhuitl. Large bumps[3] spread[4] on people; some people had pustules all over their bodies ... [The sick people] could no longer walk about, but lay in their sleeping places... And when they moved, they cried out loudly. The pustules caused[5] great suffering; very many people died of them, and many just starved[6] to death; ... and no one took care of the others any longer."

From: Excerpt and illustration from Sahagún, Historia general de las cosas de Nueva España, ca. 1575–1580

With the help of 200,000 soldiers from other Mexican cities, Cortés destroyed Tenochtitlán, with all its palaces and temples, in the name of Christianity[7] on August 12, 1521. The Spanish built a new city on top of the ruins and called it **México**. The famous Aztec temples and palaces were soon forgotten. In the 20th century, some parts of the central temple were excavated[8] and can now be found in museums. Spain ruled Mexico till 1821.

Pizarro conquered the Inca empire

In the 1530s, the Spanish captain and soldier **Francisco Pizarro** (1476 – 1541) with another small army of 300 soldiers quickly took control of the large ▸ **Inca empire** in South America. This was relatively easy because so many natives were dying of the European disease[9] **smallpox**[10]. The Spanish killed the king, the *Inca*, in 1533.

Suffering[11] in the Americas ...

After the defeat[12] of the native people in Mexico and South America, the Spanish settlers[13] owned[14] all the land. The natives who lived on this land had to work for the Spanish owners. In the Inca area (for example, Bolivia), every family had to send someone to work in the Spanish gold and silver mines[15]. When that person died, mostly after a year or two, the family had to send someone else.

The Spanish sent priests to teach the natives about Jesus Christ and make them Christians. Spanish became the official language[16] in the countries which were conquered by the Spanish.

Fifty years after the Spanish had landed, 90% of the natives of Mexico and the West Indies had died. Most natives had died because they were not immune against the diseases which the Europeans had brought with them. As a consequence[17], the Spanish did not have enough workers for their plantations and mines, so **African slaves**[18] were brought over to the ▸ **Americas**.

... wealth[19] in Spain and Europe

The empire in the Americas brought immense wealth to Spain. In 1541, the Spanish discovered ▸ **Cerro Rico** next to the city of ▸ **Potosí** in southern Bolivia – a mountain of silver. In the 1580s, nearly 300,000 kilograms of silver were shipped[20] each year. 500 ships with gold and silver arrived in Seville (*Sevilla*) in Spain each year. The result of the flood[21] of silver and gold could soon be seen in the buildings of the city, especially ▸ **Seville cathedral** – the largest in the world, 100 metres wide and 150 metres long.

1 epidemic *Epidemie*
2 pustule *Pustel*
3 bumps *Beulen*
4 to spread *sich ausbreiten*
5 to cause *verursachen*
6 to starve *verhungern*
7 Christianity *Christentum*
8 to excavate *ausgraben*
9 disease *Krankheit*
10 smallpox *Pocken*
11 suffering (n) *Leid*
12 defeat (n) *Niederlage*
13 settler *Siedler/in*
14 to own *besitzen*
15 mine *Berkwerk*
16 official language *Amtssprache*
17 as a consequence *daher, folglich, demzufolge*
18 slave *Sklave, Sklavin*
19 wealth *Wohlstand, Reichtum*
20 to ship *verschiffen, transportieren*
21 flood (n) *Flut, Überflutung*

Tasks: Old and New World

1 List the things that changed for the Native Americans after the Spanish arrived in the Americas.

2 Who did what?
a ... conquered the Aztec Empire. b Many ... died because they were not immune against ...
c The ... killed prisoners of war as a present for their ... d Cortés ... Tenochtitlán.

4.5 One of the most important years in history: 1492

The ▸ triangular trade across the Atlantic 1500–1850

In October 1492, life in the Americas, Europe and Africa changed forever.
In the following 350 years, around **15 million African men, women and children** were transported from Africa to the Americas against their will. They worked there as **slaves** on the plantations[1] of their white owners. But millions also died on their way there.
The slave trade brought great suffering to Africans, but became good business[2] for merchants in the port[3] cities of Portugal, the Netherlands, Britain, and France.
From the port cities in Europe, ships started their voyages to **West Africa** full of cloth[4], guns, alcohol, and metal goods[5]. The captains and merchants sold their goods there and bought slaves[6] from African chiefs[7] and kings. Then they took the slaves to the **Americas**, sold them and returned to Europe with gold, silver, tobacco[8], and sugar.
This trade with its typical cargo[9] connected Europe, Africa and the Americas. It is called **triangular trade across the Atlantic** (*Transatlantischer Dreieckshandel*).

S 12 ▸ Elmina Castle, Ghana, one of the 60 slave castles along the West African coast

The Portuguese built the castle in 1482 as a trade centre for gold. The castle was taken over by the Dutch in 1637. They used the building as a holding place for slaves until 1814. Each year up to 30,000 slaves were shipped to the Americas from here. The beautiful apartments of the Dutch were upstairs. The cells for the slaves were downstairs. Sometimes 200 people were in one cell for up to two months. They often did not have enough space to lie down.

Tasks: Triangular trade across the Atlantic 1500–1850

1 Copy and fill in the table. What was shipped to which continent?

From Europe to Africa	*From Africa to the Americas*	*From the Americas to Europe*

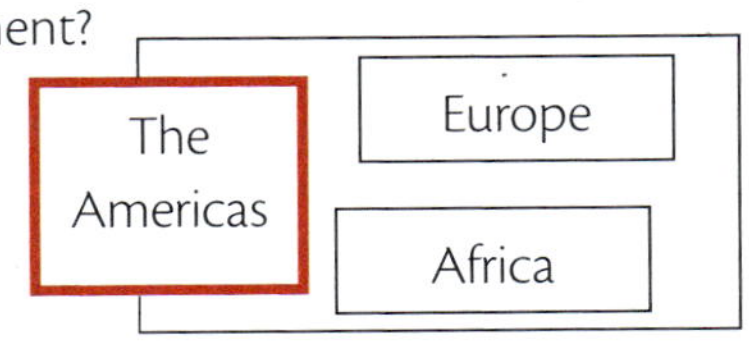

2 Copy the diagram on the right and label[10] it. Draw the route and the cargo of a ship in the triangular trade. (Where does it start? What is its cargo? Where does it go then?)

3 List the groups of people who benefited[11] from the triangular trade. Are there any people who are not mentioned in the text above?

4 Check the list of World Heritage sites on p. 89. Explain why Elmina Castle was made a World Heritage site.

1 plantation *Plantage, landwirtschaftlicher Großbetrieb in warmem Klima, auf dem zumeist ein Produkt angebaut wird*
2 business *Geschäft*
3 port *Hafen*
4 cloth *Tuch*
5 goods *Güter, Waren*
6 slave *Sklave/Sklavin*
7 chief *Häuptling, Stammesoberhaupt*
8 tobacco *Tabak*
9 cargo *Ladung*
10 (to) label *beschriften*
11 (to) benefit from sth. *von etw. profitieren, Nutzen haben*

The exchange[1] of plants, animals, and diseases between the continents

The Europeans brought a great number of animals (see **S 6** on p. 54) and plants with them to the Americas. Because of this, Native Americans could ride horses, eat the meat of pigs and drink the milk of cows for the first time.

But the Europeans also discovered animals and plants in the Americas which were new to them. They took these new **American plants** back to Europe to find out if they could grow them there too. In 1532, for example, the Spanish saw the Native Americans in Peru eating strange, round objects: **potatoes**. Thirty years later they took potatoes to Spain. But it took Europeans 200 years to find out that potatoes were healthy and could feed millions of people. Potatoes helped to fight hunger in Europe.

Many people, plants and animals of the **Old and the New World**[2] began to mix after 1492. This changed the way of life on all three continents:

- People started eating new kinds[3] of food.
- Europeans had more food so the population there grew.
- Native Americans discovered a new way of hunting[4] using European horses.
- The landscape[5] changed because forests, for example, were cut down[6] to make room for the sugar plantations.

S 13 The exchange of plants, animals and diseases between the continents after 1492

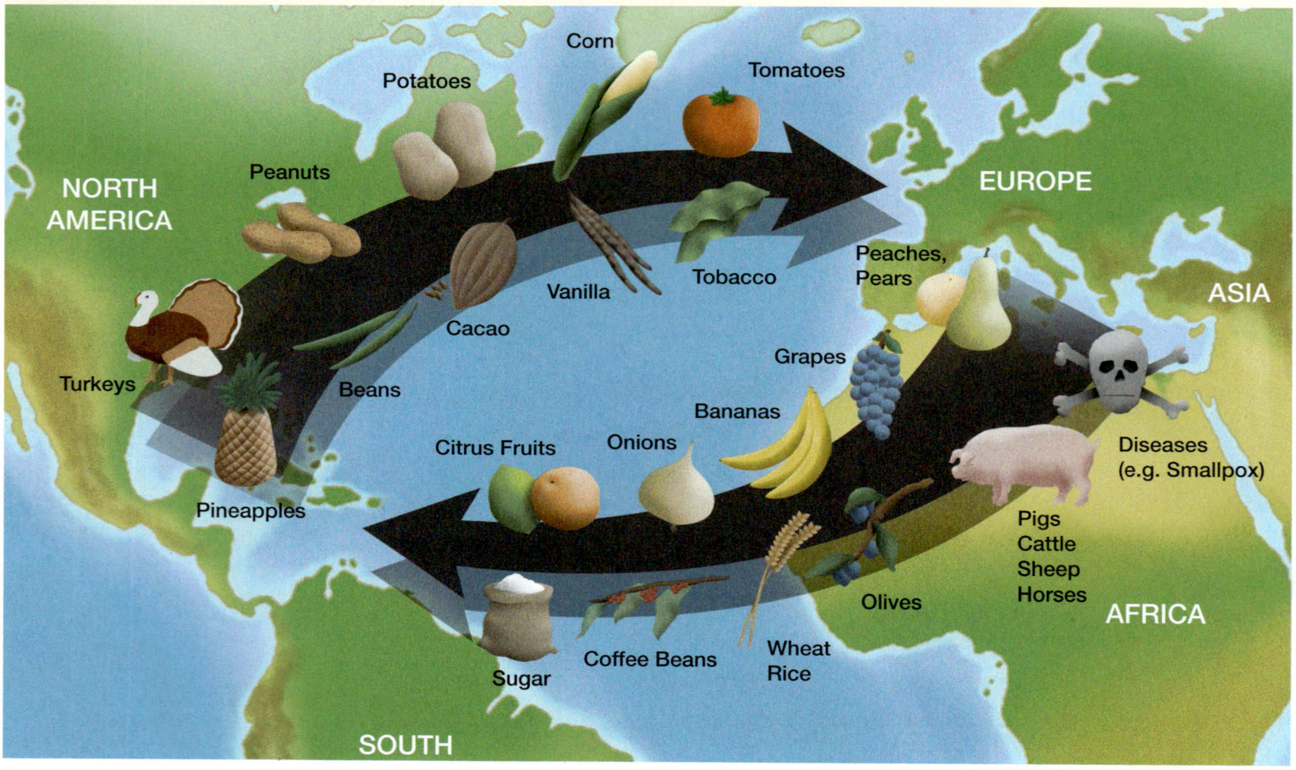

1 exchange *Austausch*
2 Old World *die Alte Welt = Europa*
New World *die Neue Welt = Amerika*
3 a kind of *eine Art von*
4 to hunt *jagen*
5 landscape *Landschaft*
6 to cut down *fällen, abholzen*
7 dish *Gericht, Speise*

Tasks: Exchanges between the continents

1 Study **S 13**. Identify what the Europeans brought with them besides plants and animals.

2 List three of your favourite dishes[7]. Could you eat them today if the Europeans had not brought American fruits and vegetables to Europe?

3 List three dishes which people in the Americas could not eat if the Europeans had not brought animals, fruits and vegetables form the Old World to the Americas.

4 Explain why 1492 was an important year for Africans, Native Americans and Europeans. Who benefited most? Give your reasons.

Unit revision

The Age of Discovery

S 14 **Aztec warrior**

It all began with old legends ...

Key terms

Age of Discovery • direct route to India • slave trade • Aztec and Inca Empires • Tenochtitlán • the Americas • smallpox

History skills

Making timelines • identifying sources • analysing historical maps and diagrams

Activate your English

Describing charts and historical maps • time phrases

Key personalities

Paolo Toscanelli • Christopher Columbus • Prince Henry • Hernán Cortés • Moctezuma II

S 15 **African slaves on a sugar plantation**

Revision tasks: The Age of Discovery

1 Write the Aztec warrior's story about how the Aztec army was defeated and what happened to Tenochtitlán. ***Language help:*** *It all began with old legends which....*

2 Explain why these slaves from Africa are working on a sugar plantation.

3 Explain the terms 'Old World' and 'New World'.

4 Project work: Copy the chart and fill it in.

	Your answer in note form
why explorers went on dangerous voyages	
who supported them and why	*Who:* *Motives:*
what technical developments made it possible	
who and what they found	
what the effects on the people in Europe, Africa and the Americas were	*People in Europe:* *Africa:* *The Americas:*

5 Share your chart with a partner/group and make changes so that everybody has the same version. Then write a short text for a 2-minute presentation called "The Age of Discovery". ***Language help:*** *During the Age of Discovery, explorers went on dangerous voyages because ...*

5.1 Martin Luther and his criticism

S1 Martin Luther, Wittenberg 1529, painting by Lucas Cranach

Can you buy your way out of purgatory?

In 1517, a German monk[1] called **Johann Tetzel** (1460–1519), began to sell so-called ▸ **letters of indulgence**[2] in the area around the city of Magdeburg. The Catholic Church promised that buying the letters would make people's time in purgatory[3] shorter. Purgatory was the horrible place where people believed they would be sent after death for the bad things (= their sins) which they had done in their lives.

Tetzel made a lot of money with the letters because people were afraid. Most of this money went to **Albrecht, the new Archbishop**[4] **of Mainz and Magdeburg.** He needed the money because he had to pay **Pope**[5] **Leo X** in Rome to get his position as archbishop. The Pope on the other hand needed the money because he wanted to build the new ▸ **St. Peter's Basilica** (*Petersdom*) in Rome.

Martin Luther – the beginning of the Reformation

Late in 1517, ▸ **Martin Luther** (1483–1546), the young monk and professor of theology[6] (the study of God and ideas about God) at the new university of Wittenberg in Saxony (*Sachsen*), wrote a letter to Archbishop Albrecht. He strongly criticized[7] the idea that all people needed was a letter of indulgence from the Pope and they would go straight to heaven after their death. For Luther it was clear that people only went to heaven if they believed in God. Luther sent the Archbishop **95 theses**[8] (a list of detailed points in Latin) to explain his ideas. To start a discussion, he also sent them to some bishops and a few friends. Till the end of 1517, copies of the 95 theses were translated[9] from Latin into German and printed in different German cities. Luther became a famous man. From then on, it was not only priests and monks who were discussing Luther's ideas, but also the common people[10]. The most shocking thing for the Archbishop and the Pope in Rome was that many people in Germany agreed with Luther.

Luther became an outlaw

Albrecht was very angry with Luther because the people had stopped buying the letters of indulgence. So he decided to destroy[11] him and Luther had to defend[12] himself. However, he did not take back what he had said. He criticized even more things which he believed were wrong with the Church. As a result, the Pope ▸ **excommunicated**[13] Luther in 1521. This meant that he was not a member of the Church any longer. People believed that he would go to hell when he died. Nobody was allowed to have anything to do with him.

In 1521 **Emperor Charles V** (*Karl der Fünfte*, 1500–1558) of the ▸ **Holy Roman Empire of the German Nation** (*Heiliges Römisches Reich Deutscher Nation*) ordered[14] Luther to visit the **Diet of Worms** (*Reichstag zu Worms*), a meeting of the rulers[15] of the Empire. There Luther defended his ideas again and did not take back what he had said. Therefore, the Emperor declared Luther an outlaw[16], which meant he could be arrested[17] and killed by everyone. It was forbidden to print, buy, or sell Luther's books and writings. However, **Frederick III** (*Friedrich*, 1463–1525), the ruler of Saxony, did not obey[18] the Emperor. He secretly[19] took Luther to one of his castles, the ▸ **Wartburg**, near Eisenach. There Luther was safe and **translated the Bible**[20] into German.

1 monk *Mönch*
2 indulgence *Ablass*
3 purgatory *Fegefeuer*
4 (Arch)bishop *(Erz-) Bischof*
5 pope *Papst*
6 theology *Theologie*
7 to criticize sb. *jmdn. kritisieren*
8 thesis, pl theses *These, Thesen*
9 to translate *übersetzen*
10 common people *einfache Bevölkerung*
11 to destroy sb. *jmdn. vernichten*
12 to defend sb./sth. *jmdn./etw. verteidigen*
13 to excommunicate *exkommunizieren, aus der Kirche ausschließen*
14 to order *befehlen*
15 ruler *hier: Herrscher*
16 to declare sb. an outlaw *jmdn. zu einem Ausgestoßenen erklären*
17 to arrest *verhaften*
18 to obey *gehorchen*
19 secretly (adv.) *insgeheim*
20 Bible *Bibel*

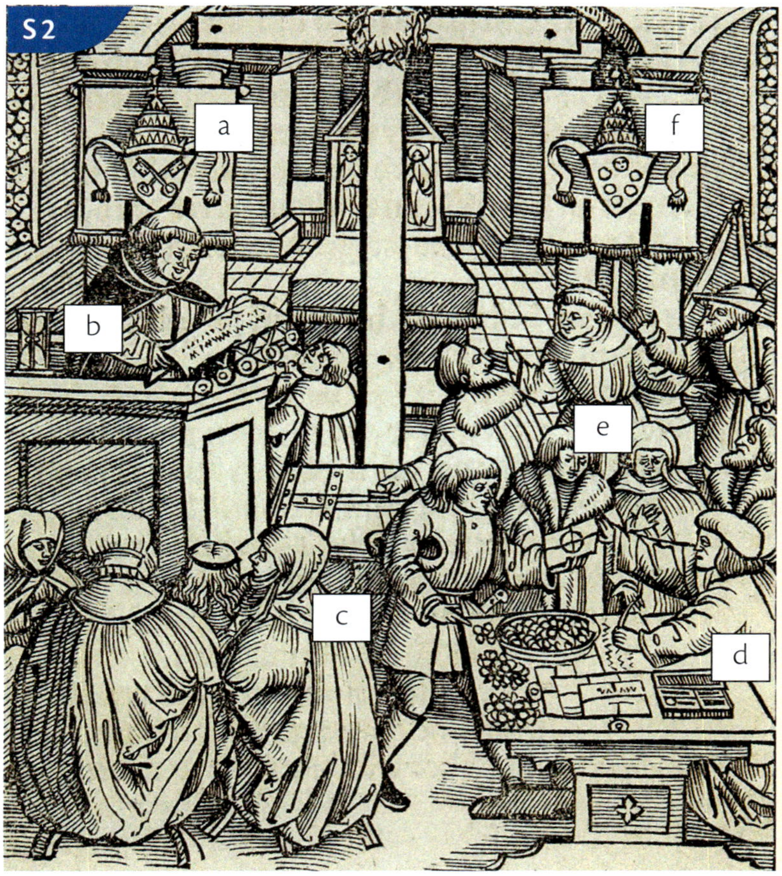

***Ablasshandel* (trade with letters of indulgence), print[1] by Heinrich Vogtherr der Ältere, Augsburg, 1521**

This print was on the cover[2] of the pamphlet[3] *"Beklagung eines Laien, genannt Hans Schwalb, über viele Missbräuche christlichen Lebens"* (The complaint of a layman, called Hans Schwalb, about the many things a Christian can do wrong in his life).

This print shows the inside of a church:

1 The chest[4] for the indulgence money is under the cross.
2 A man is giving the letters to buyers.
3 A priest is blessing[5] two men. One of them is putting money into the chest.
4 A monk is reading a letter written by the pope who allows the selling of indulgences.
5 Two flags showing: the arms[6] of Pope Leo X is on the left.
6 The flag of the pope's family is on the right.

Tasks: Luther and the letters of indulgence

1 Who does what? Copy the table and fill it in.

	Who was this person?	*What did he do?*	*Why did he do it?*
Tetzel			
Luther			
Albrecht			
Leo X			
Charles V			
Frederick III			

2 Read the caption of **S 2** carefully. Copy the table and fill in:

Who made the source?	*When and where?*	*Where could people find it?*

3 Match the letters in the boxes in **S 2** to the correct sentences found in the source caption.

4 Which of the following sentences best expresses the message[7] of **S 2**? (Hint[8]: Think of the title of the pamphlet.)

a The sale of letters of indulgence is ok.
b Churches are full because many people want to buy letters of indulgence.
c Selling letters of indulgence is one of the many wrong things in a Christian life.
d Churches have become shops.

1 print (n)/to print *Druck/drucken*
2 cover *Titelseite*
3 pamphlet *Broschüre, Flugblatt, Pamphlet*
4 chest *Truhe*
5 to bless *segnen*
6 arms *hier: Wappen*
7 message *Botschaft, Aussage*
8 hint *Hinweis*

5.2 Luther's ideas changed Germany

Chaos in Germany

Luther's ideas and his attack on the Catholic Church changed Germany. Monasteries[1] and convents[2] closed because monks and nuns[3] left them. Paintings in churches were destroyed. People said that they did not need priests any longer because they were able to read the Bible in German. So priests who wanted to stay with the Catholic Church were driven out of town. Some radicals thought that changing the Church was just the beginning. They also wanted to change much more. Why not take power[4] and wealth away from the rich monasteries and noble[5] lords?

The peasants[6] rebelled[7]

In 1525, the news from Southern Germany seemed unbelievable. Poor townspeople stopped paying their taxes[8]. Peasants stormed the castles[9] of their lords, looted[10] them and set them on fire. They demanded[11] freedom[12] and justice[13]. Did Luther not say that all people were equal[14] before God? How was it possible then that many peasants were not free people and had to pay unfair taxes? Was it fair that noble lords could take away more and more of their land and their rights?

S 3 **Jacob Murer, *Flucht* (flight), drawing, 1525**

Murer, abbot[15] of Weißenau, wrote about and drew the events[16] in the *Weißenauer Chronik des Bauernkrieges*. The abbot described and made drawings of how the peasants stormed and looted the monastery.

The revenge[17] of the rulers: The Peasants' War[18] of 1525

At first Luther showed sympathy with the demands of the peasants, but when they became more and more violent he told the rulers to crush[19] the peasants' rebellion. Their military leaders[20] did this in an extremely bloody way in May 1525. Altogether around 100,000 peasants died in the fights. The leaders of the peasants were cruelly[21] executed[22].

Tasks: The peasants rebelled and the rulers took revenge

1 Identify the reasons why the peasants rebelled in 1525.

2 Describe drawing **S 3**. What are the buildings on the right? Who do you think is fleeing and who are the men with pikes[23]? ***Language help:*** *The drawing by ... shows ....*

3 Give possible reasons why the rulers and their armies could quickly crush the peasants' rebellion.

1 monastery *Männerkloster*
2 convent *Frauenkloster*
3 nun *Nonne*
4 power *Macht*
5 noble (n, adj.) *Adlige/r, adlig*
6 peasant *(mittelalterliche/r Bauer/Bäuerin*
7 to rebel *sich auflehnen, rebellieren*
8 tax *Steuer*
9 castle *Burg, Schloss*
10 to loot *plündern*
11 (to) demand (n, v) *Forderung, fordern*
12 freedom *Freiheit*
13 justice *Gerechtigkeit*
14 equal *gleich*
15 abbot *Abt*
16 event *Ereignis*
17 revenge *Rache*
18 Peasants' War *Bauernkrieg*
19 to crush *zerschlagen*
20 leader *Anführer/in*
21 cruel *grausam*
22 to execute *hinrichten*
23 pike *Spieß*

5.3 Printing and spreading Luther's ideas

Before the middle of the 15th century, all books were written by hand. This made them very expensive and very few people could afford[1] them. But more and more people wanted to buy books. Therefore many inventors[2] tried to find a way to produce books more cheaply and in great numbers.
Around 1450, ▸ **Johannes Gutenberg** of Mainz (ca. 1400–1468) began to print words on paper. He cut letters into metal and fitted them together to make words. Then he put ink[3] on them and pressed them down on paper. With his new invention he could produce identical copies of the same page quickly and correctly. In 1455 he printed his first book: the Bible.

Printing was so successful that in the year 1500 there were already 1120 printing shops in 250 cities in Europe. They printed, for example, stories of discoveries in the Americas or medical texts. All of them could use pictures and illustrations.

Since bookmaking was much cheaper, more people could buy books. Information spread faster and more easily. It has been estimated that there were perhaps 30,000 books in all of Europe before Gutenberg printed his Bible; 50 years later, there were 20 million books.
The printing press[4] turned Martin Luther into a best-selling author and helped spread his message. One-page pamphlets with his teachings[5] were printed. Travelling salesmen sold them cheaply and quickly in Germany and the rest of Europe. Millions of people learned about his ideas when the pamphlets were passed around[6] and talked about after church or in the market places. Most of the pamphlets were interesting to look at because they contained[7] pictures which made fun of Luther's enemies.

S4 **Gutenberg's printing press**

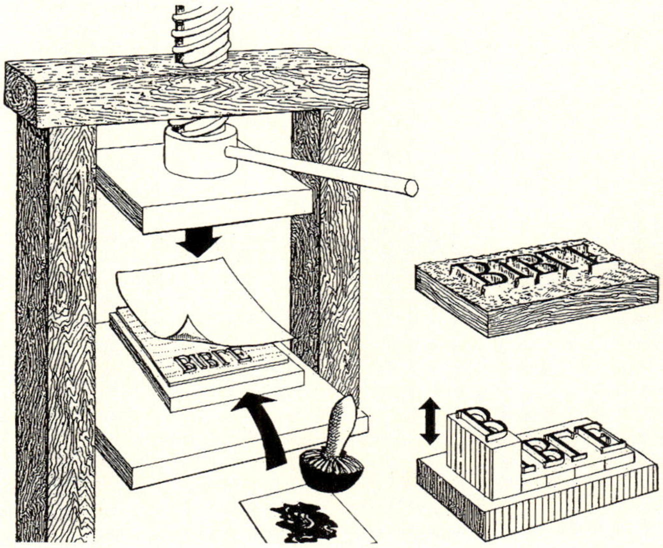

S5

In 1542, a German historian[8] called Johann Sleidan, proudly said:
"A new art[9] was invented in our land, the art of printing. Each man became eager[10] for knowledge[11] and felt very surprised about his former[12] blindness."

From: Elizabeth L. Eisenstein, The Printing Revolution in Early Modern Europe, New York 2005, p. 167

Activate your English

Talking about effects

because of sth.	*wegen etwas*
have the effect	*die Wirkung/den Effekt haben*
therefore	*deswegen*
as a result/consequence, consequently	*folglich, dementsprechend*

Tasks: An invention and its effects

1 The printing press was invented around 1450.
  a List five effects which this had.
  b Write five sentences using the expressions in the Activate your English box: "Talking about effects".

2 Tell your partner what Johann Sleidan wrote about the new invention (**S 5**). What was he expecially proud[13] of?

1 to afford sth. *sich etw. leisten*
2 inventor/invention *Erfinder/in/Erfindung*
3 ink *Tinte*
4 printing press *Druckerpresse*
5 teaching *Lehre*
6 to pass sth. around *etw. herumreichen*
7 to contain *enthalten*
8 historian *Historiker/in*
9 art/artist *Kunst/Künstler/in*
10 eager for sth. *begierig auf etw.*
11 knowledge *Wissen*
12 former *frühere, früherer, früheres*
13 proud *stolz*

Analysing cartoons[1]

S6 **The title: *"Der Papstesel zu Rom"* (The donkey pope of Rome)**

The artist: Lukas Cranach

The place where the woodcut was made: Wittenberg

The time when the woodcut was made: 1523

Pictures as weapons[2]

The pictures on the Reformation pamphlets were the most interesting part for most people – especially for those who could not read. Consequently, Lutherans[3] (followers[4] of Luther), as well as the Catholic Church used the pictures to attack each other.

They showed people as monsters, demons, devils, or with animal heads. Sometimes they compared Luther's teachings with the Pope's, the new Church with the old. People at the time could recognize[5] the persons in the cartoon because of their typical haircuts (for example, monks), clothes, hats, their flags and the things which they had in their hands. Today, these types of pictures are called **cartoons**.

Some examples of the messages of the cartoons were
- that the Pope and the bishops were are only interested in money or
- that Luther's teachings were are the invention of the devil.

Today it is sometimes impossible to understand the cartoons because we do not always know the meaning[6] of some of the objects[7] or the animals. Could they be symbols and stand for something else?

History skills	Activate your English
Artist/Title: What is the title of the cartoon? Who made the cartoon? When and where was it made?	*The cartoon is called ...* *The cartoon was created[8] by ... in ... (place) in ... (time).*
Describe: Describe the people, animals, objects and/or activities that are shown.	*The cartoon shows ... in the centre/on the right/on the left/at the bottom/in the foreground/ background ...*
Explain who or what the people/animals/ objects are: Do the people/animals have typical characteristics[9] which help the audience[10] to understand who or what they are? What do the animals/people/actions/objects stand for[11]?	*The ... stand(s) for/symbolize(s)/mean(s) ... because ...* *The cartoonist shows ... which mean(s) that ...*
The cartoonist's message: What does the cartoon/cartoonist want to tell his/her/its audience?	*... (name of cartoon/cartoonist) wants to tell his/her/its audience that ...*

1 cartoon *Karikatur, Spottbild*
2 weapon *Waffe*
3 Lutheran *Lutheraner/in*
4 follower *Anhänger/in, Jünger/in*
5 to recognize *erkennen*
6 meaning *Bedeutung*
7 object *Gegenstand*
8 to create sth. *etw. (er)schaffen*
9 characteristic *Kennzeichen, Eigenschaft*
10 audience *Leserschaft, Zuschauer*
11 to stand for sth. *etw. bedeuten, für etw. stehen*

S 7 ***"Luthers und Luzifers einträchtige Vereinigung"*** **(Luther's and Lucifer's [= the devil's] peaceful union), unknown artist, woodcut, Leipzig, 1535**

S 8 **"Anti-Passional", Lucas Cranach, woodcut, Wittenberg, 1521**

Task:
Analyse the two cartoons – **S 7** and **S 8**.

5.4 Faith divided Germany

From protest to a Protestant Church

Luther and his teachings were banned[1] after the **Diet of Worms** in 1521 (see p. 60). However, many Germans did not obey[2] the ban[3] because they liked Luther's teachings. Others did not obey the ban because their rulers forced them to believe the things Luther taught.

As a result, most of the princes of the German lands who stayed Catholic formed an alliance[4]. At the next diet in Speyer in 1529, they demanded that everybody had to obey the ban. However, Luther's followers protested. They were in the minority[5] and, from then on, they were called **"Protestants"**.

At the diet at Augsburg in 1530, the Protestants explained their beliefs[6]. **Emperor Charles V**, however, wanted everybody to practise the same religion[7]. Therefore he argued that the Protestants' beliefs were wrong and that they had to become Catholic again. The Protestant rulers did not do this and formed an alliance against the emperor in 1531. From then on, Germany was divided into two Churches[8].

War and peace

When the Emperor wanted to force[9] the Protestants to become Catholic again, he began a war and defeated them in 1547. But at the Diet of Augsburg in 1555, Catholic and Protestant rulers signed[10] **The Peace of Augsburg** (*Augsburger Religionsfrieden*) with the following terms[11]:

- The rulers could choose their religion.
- The rulers had the right to decide[12] the religion of the people who lived in their states.
- Those people who did not want to practise the religion of their rulers had to emigrate[13].

S9 **Christian Europe was divided in 1570**

Tasks: Christian Europe was divided

1. Read the terms of the Peace of Augsburg above. Are the following sentences right or wrong?
   a The rulers in the German states had to practise the religion of the emperor.
   b People could move to a state where *their* religion was practised.
   c In each German state there was only one religion after 1555.
   d The people in each state could freely choose which religion they wanted to practise.
   e People were not persecuted[14] because of their religion.
2. Study the map **S9**. Which parts of Europe became Protestant and which parts stayed Catholic?

1 to ban sth. *verbieten*
2 to obey *gehorchen*
3 ban (n.) *offizielles Verbot*
4 to form an alliance *ein Bündnis schließen*
5 minority *Minderheit*
6 belief *Glauben, Überzeugung*
7 to practise a religion *eine Religion ausüben*
8 Churches *hier: Konfessionen (religiöse Gruppen innerhalb einer Religion)*
9 to force *zwingen*
10 to sign *unterzeichnen*
11 terms *Bestimmungen (in einem Vertrag)*
12 to decide *entscheiden*
13 to emigrate *auswandern*
14 to persecute sb. *jmdn. verfolgen*

5.5 The Protestant Reformation spread in Europe

Reformers and Protestant Reformation in different countries

Luther's ideas quickly became well known in other countries in Europe. Soon there were Lutheran Churches in Switzerland, France, Denmark, Norway, Sweden, Scotland and the Netherlands. In some countries, the rulers wanted the changes and in others, like in France and the Netherlands, they were against them. As a consequence, there were decades[1] of bloody fights in France.

But the new Lutherans did not accept all of Luther's ideas. They often had their own ideas. The Swiss pastors **Ulrich Zwingli** (1484–1531) and **Johannes Calvin** (1509–1564) were, for example, more radical than Luther. In Zurich (*Zürich*), Zwingli thought that all true Christian people had to do exactly what the Bible told them. Because of that, the city council[2] in Zurich tried to control the lives of its citizens to make them good Christians.

Can cities become Cities of God?

Calvin wanted to make **Geneva** (*Genf*) a "City of God", where reformed Christians could live safely. Even the government had to obey the laws of God. Townspeople were taught to lead[3] a Christian life. They were punished[4] if they did not. In 1546, pubs were made illegal. Dancing was forbidden in 1550. The pastors had the right to visit people at home to make sure that they were living a Christian life. But not all people accepted this so they complained[5] about this control. These people were thrown out of the city and some were even executed.

A school was built to teach theology. Geneva's school of theology became famous in Europe. Many young men from France, England and the Netherlands came to study there and took Calvin's teachings back home. As a result, Calvin's influence in these countries was even greater than Luther's.

S 10 ***Das Zürcherische Sittenmandat, 1530***

Wir gebieten, dass jedermann ohne Ausnahme, der sich nicht durch Krankheit oder andere ehrliche Gründe bei der Gemeinde oder beim Pfarrer entschuldigen kann, alle Sonntage bei guter Zeit zur Kirche gehe und bis zu Ende verbleibe. ... Kein Wirt darf Einheimischen an Sonn- und Feiertagen vor der Predigt Speise und Trank geben. Kein Einheimischer soll sich nachts nach 9 Uhr mehr im Wirtshause finden lassen .... so haben wir auf das Ansuchen (Bitten) unsrer Landleute alle Spiele verboten, es sei mit Karten, Würfeln, Brettspiel, Kegeln, Wetten usw.

From: Meltzer, Hermann, Kirchengeschichtliches Quellenlesebuch, Dresden-Blasewitz 1917

Luther and the reformers in Switzerland could never overcome their differences[6]. Because of this, different Protestant Churches developed. Zwingli and Calvin's Church was called the "**Reformed Church**" (*Reformierte Kirche*) and Luther's the "**Lutheran Church**" (*Lutherische Kirche*).

Calvin's followers in England, who were called "**Puritans**" (*Puritaner*), felt that they could not practise their religion freely. Therefore they left England. They were the first people who took Calvin's teachings to North America in 1620.

Tasks: Cities of God

1 Imagine[7] it is 1530 and you are writing to a friend in England about what is forbidden in Zurich. (**S 10**). ***Language help:*** *It is forbidden to ... People must/must not ...* (Do not translate the text word for word.) Write about why you like or do not like the new rules.

2 Role play: Imagine you are a member of the Zurich city council. Write down some arguments to defend/attack the strict laws.

3 Discuss why the ideas of Zwingli and Calvin were attractive for many people.

1 decade *Jahrzehnt*
2 city council *Stadtrat*
3 to lead, led, led *führen*
4 to punish *bestrafen*
5 to complain *sich beschweren*
6 to overcome differences *hier: Meinungsverschiedenheiten überwinden*
7 to imagine sth. *sich etw. vorstellen*

5.6 Faith and power – thirty years of war

The Thirty Years' War: enemies and causes

The **Thirty Years' War** (*Dreißigjähriger Krieg*) was a very complicated **series[1] of wars** which were fought in the **Holy Roman Empire** between 1618–1648.

Why did the war start? It started because of the **tensions[2] between Catholics and Protestants.** At the beginning of the 17th century, the relationship[3] between Catholic and Protestant rulers in Germany became so bad that both sides formed military alliances.

The **spark[4]** that started the war came in 1618 when Protestants protested that they could not practise their religion freely. In the Hradčany (*Hradschin*) Castle in Prague, leaders threw two of the Emperor's Catholic governors[5] out of the window (*Prager Fenstersturz*). Nobody thought at that moment that this protest would lead to an international conflict and thirty years of war.

The Thirty Years' War was a war between Catholic and Protestant rulers in Europe:

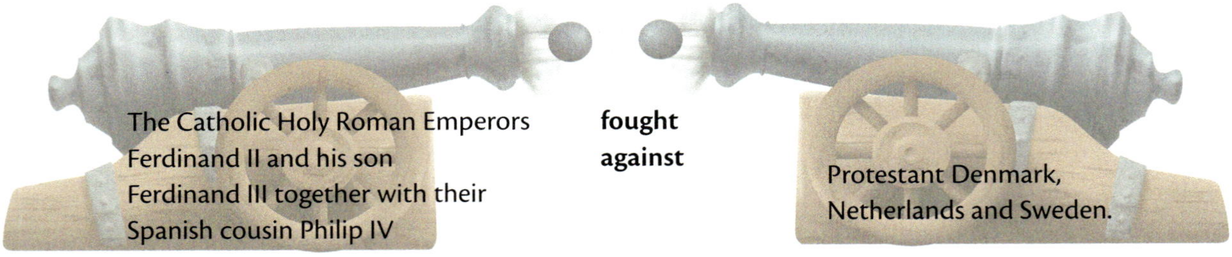

Motives:
to crush the Protestants and win more power over the German princes in the Holy Roman Empire

Motives:
to support the Protestants in the Holy Roman Empire, to conquer parts of the Empire, and to prevent[6] the growth[7] of power of the German emperor in Europe

It was also a war between different German states:

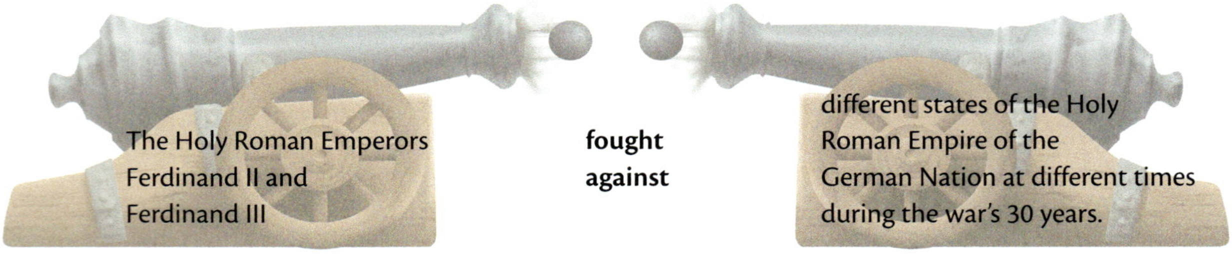

War was their business

The soldiers of the armies in this war came from all over Europe. They fought for the general who could pay best. Consequently, they were not really interested in peace because war meant they had work.
People had to pay more and more taxes to pay the armies. At the same time people had to give away their food and cattle so that the soldiers had something to eat.
If the soldiers did not get what they wanted, they used force[8]. They ruined villages, towns and castles. Looting[9] was normal. Starvation and diseases followed. The war became a nightmare[10] for the people.

1 series *Serie, Abfolge*
2 tensions *Spannungen*
3 relationship *Beziehung*
4 spark *Zündfunke*
5 governor *hier: Statthalter*
6 to prevent *verhindern*
7 growth *Wachstum*
8 to use force *Gewalt anwenden*
9 to loot *plündern*
10 nightmare *Alptraum*

Peace[1] after thirty years

After decades of fighting[2] it became clear to all parties that the war could not be won. Therefore, peace talks[3] began in 1643. However, it took five years till the **Peace of Westphalia** *(Westfälischer Frieden)* was signed[4] in Münster and Osnabrück in 1648.

The **winners** were

- **France and Sweden**, which had both conquered parts of Germany and became more powerful in Europe as a result.
- the **German princes**, who became more powerful and more independent[5] from the Holy Roman Emperor.

S 11 **Population losses[6] in the Holy Roman Empire during the Thirty Years' War**

Around 18 million people lived in the Holy Roman Empire in 1618. It is estimated that the population was 30 per cent[7] smaller in 1648.

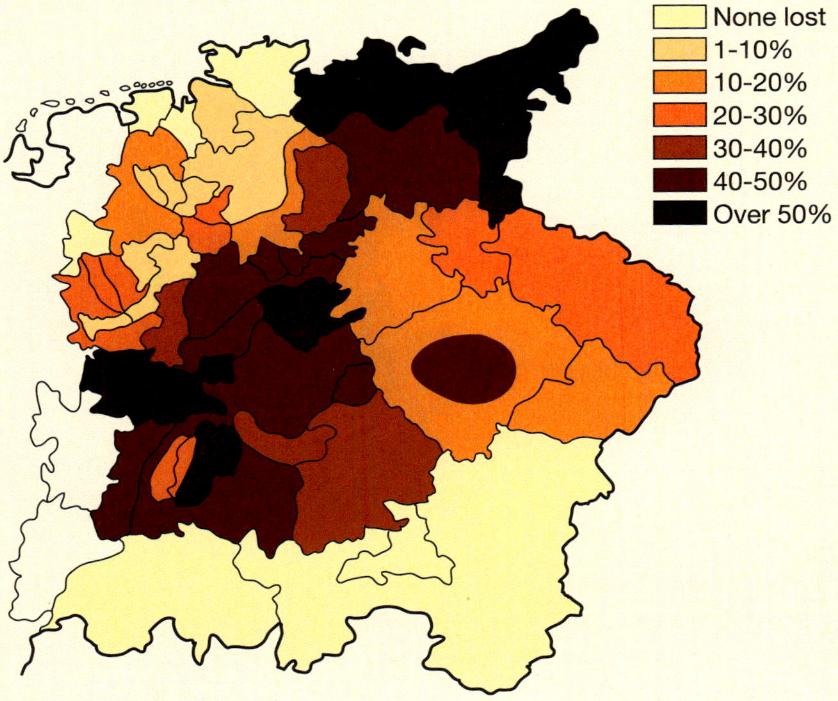

Tasks: Thirty years of war

1 Collect facts about the Thirty Years' War on pp. 68–69. Copy the table and fill it in.

When did it begin and end?	
Where was it fought?	
How did it end?	
Why did the war break out?	
Who fought?	
What were the effects? (**S 9, 10, 11**)	

Compare your findings with a partner/group and make changes. Then write an article about *The Thirty Years' War*. Begin like this: *The Thirty Years' War began in … and ended in …*

2 Look for the area of your hometown on the map. How many per cent of the population were lost during the war (**S 11**)?

1 peace *Frieden*
2 to fight, fought, fought *(be-)kämpfen*
3 peace talks *Friedensgespräche*
4 to sign *unterzeichnen*
5 independent *unabhängig*
6 population loss *Bevölkerungsverlust*
7 per cent *Prozent*

War and its victims

S 12 Maurus Friesenegger, a Catholic monk, described the looting of a Bavarian monastery and its village[1] in 1633 by Protestant soldiers:

The village, where the soldiers found only empty houses and no people, looked terrible. The whole village seemed to be on fire. They took chairs and benches out of the houses, pulled down roofs and had dangerous fires in the street. They shouted and screamed because they were hungry and frustrated. Nobody from the village who was watching from far away had any hope of seeing his house again. On the next day the hungry soldiers searched[2] the woods and found enough hidden[3] food to still their hunger.

From: http://www.mtholyoke.edu/courses/rschwart/hist260/30YrsWar.htm

Many soldiers fighting in the Thirty Year's War did not wear uniforms. They wore civilian clothes[4]. Especially at the end of the war, the generals did not have any money to pay for uniforms. Without uniforms, it was sometimes hard for the soldiers and even the generals to identify who their friends and enemies were.

We can only recognize the soldiers in **S 13** because of their sword and horse. The people in the print without these things were peasants.

S 13 Hans Ulrich Franck, *"Kriegsgräuel"* (The horrors of war), Augsburg, print, 1655

S 14 A report about the attack and looting of Nördlingen, a Protestant city, by a Protestant army in 1634

[...] because we did not regard[5] him as an enemy and there were no warnings to regard his army as an enemy, we had hidden nothing. But Duke Bernhard's troops[6] broke into our land and took away our horses, cattle, bread, flour[7], salt, linen[8], clothes and everything we owned. They were brutal to the people, shooting, stabbing[9], and beating a number of people to death.

From: http://www.mtholyoke.edu/courses/rschwart/hist260/30YrsWar.htm

1 village *Dorf*
2 to search *durchsuchen*
3 hidden *versteckt*
4 civilian clothes *Zivilkleidung*
5 to regard *betrachten*
6 troops *Truppen*
7 flour *Mehl*
8 linen *Bettwäsche*
9 to stab *niederstechen*

Tasks: War and its victims

1 Describe what the soldiers did when they arrived at a town or village (**S 12** and **14**).
2 Identify the "mistake" the townspeople of Nördlingen made (**S 14**).
3 Describe the drawing **S 13** to your partner. Who are the people and what is going on?
Language help: legs are tied with a rope, to lift a sword, a bundle, a herd ...
4 Find possible reasons why the population losses in some areas were higher than in others.

5.7 The Holy Roman Empire of the German Nation

S 15 **The Holy Roman Empire of the German Nation around 1547**

The Holy Roman Empire was a large number of independent states

The **Holy Roman Empire of the German Nation** (*Heiliges Römisches Reich Deutscher Nation*) at the time of the Reformation was a large number of independent states. Some were larger, like Austria and Bavaria (*Österreich, Bayern*), but many of them were small, like the Duchy[1] of Berg. Then there were some that were even smaller, like the territories of the imperial knights (*Reichsritter*), who ruled over sometimes only one village. Each of these states was an independent[2] state with its own laws, currency[3], weights[4] and measures[5].

Consequently, the Holy Roman Empire did not have a capital city like Berlin, Paris or London. People did not say: "We are Germans." But they said: "We are from Saxony[6]/Hesse[7]/Brandenburg." They spoke different German dialects and even other languages like Polish[8], Czech[9], Dutch, Italian and French.

The head of the Holy Roman Empire was the **Holy Roman Emperor**. He was elected by the seven most important rulers of the Holy Roman Empire. For many centuries, the Archduke[10] of Austria[11] from the Habsburg family was elected[12] as Emperor.

The Emperor at the time of the Reformation did not have any power over the different independent states. He only had symbolic authority. His influence came mainly from the fact that he was a powerful German ruler with the largest state in the Holy Roman Empire. The princes of the Holy Roman Empire sometimes met at the **Imperial Diet** (*Reichstag*) in different cities to discuss and to decide[13] on important questions. In the end, however, the individual[14] states decided what to do.

1 duchy *Herzogtum*
2 independent *unabhängig*
3 currency *Währung*
4 weight *Gewicht*
5 measure *Maß, Maßeinheit*
6 Saxony *Sachsen*
7 Hesse *Hessen*
8 Polish *polnisch*
9 Czech *tschechisch*
10 Archduke *Erzherzog*
11 Austria *Österreich*
12 to elect *wählen*
13 to decide on sth. *über etwas entscheiden*
14 individual *einzeln*

Describing change and development with historical maps

History skills	Activate your English
Development and change What does the first/second map show us about the historical situation?	*We learn about the development of …* *The first/second map shows …* *The area/region of … is shown to be part of / under the control of / belong to / …* *At that time … was part of …* *We can see that … was divided up into …* *As the first map shows …* *During the time of …*
Which changes can you see?	*A century/decade later/ … years later* *Later … / At the beginning / in the middle / at the end of the … century* *During this period / the period from … to …, …* *After the … the situation in … had completely/hardly changed*

S 16 **The Holy Roman Empire of the German Nation around 1648**

Task:
Describe the changes and developments in the Holy Roman Empire of the German Nation between 1547 and 1648 (**S 15, 16**).

Unit revision

Reformation and Conflict

Activate your English

Describing effects

History skills

Analysing cartoons • identifying causes and effects

Key terms

Age of Reformation • letters of indulgence • Diet of Worms • Peasants' War • Thirty Years' War • Peace of Westphalia

Key personalities

Martin Luther • Johann Tetzel • Emperor Charles V • Pope Leo X • Ulrich Zwingli • Johannes Calvin • Johannes Gutenberg

Revision tasks: Reformation and Conflict

1 Copy the beginning of the sentences into your history folder and finish them. Try not to look at the text in this unit.
   a Johann Tetzel sold …
   b People believed that they would be sent to purgatory after their death because …
   c Martin Luther criticized that …
   d Charles V ordered that …
   e Luther did not …
   f Charles V banned Luther. As a consequence, …
   g Frederick III of Saxony saved Luther and took him to …, where he …

2 List three effects of Luther's criticism of the Church.

3 Tell your partner
   a why the invention of the printing press was so important for Luther.
   b how the Protestant Church got its name.
   c when the Protestant Church was made legal.
   d why there were complaints against the city council in Zurich.
   e who and which countries were active in the Thirty Years' War.
   f why so many people lost their lives in the Thirty Years' War.

4 List ten different groups of people and their actions in this unit.

Groups of people	***Their actions***
People around Magdeburg	*bought letters of indulgence.*
Luther's enemies	*wanted to …*
Monks and nuns	…
The nobles	…
The peasants	…
…	…

Louis XIV and the Age of Absolutism

6.1 The Palace of Versailles and Louis XIV

The Palace of Versailles with the garden in the background

a The King's apartment
b The Hall of Mirrors is on the garden front side of the palace. The garden front of the palace is 400 meters long from one end to the other. It has 375 windows.
c The palace chapel

The Hall of Mirrors (*Spiegelsaal*)

When the hall was finished in 1682, the visitors thought it was the most beautiful room in the palace because of its paintings, golden statues, and 357 mirrors which doubled the light from the big windows. 8,000 candles lit[1] the 73-metre-long room on ball nights.

The Palace of Versailles

For hundreds of years the French Kings lived in their palaces along the river Loire and in Paris. Then in 1682, ▸ **Louis XIV** (*Ludwig der Vierzehnte*, 1638–1715) moved his court[2] and the government[3] to the Palace of Versailles, 20 kilometres southwest of Paris. Tens of thousands of men worked more than 27 years to build the palace. This cost an enormous sum of money.
With 700 rooms, it became Europe's largest and most splendid[4] royal[5] palace at the time. But it was not only the home of the royal family. It also had hundreds of rooms for the highest-ranking[6] French nobles[7], their servants[8] and soldiers. Sometimes up to 20,000 people lived in its crowded[9] rooms.

1 to light, lit, lit *erleuchten*
2 court *Hofstaat*
3 government *Regierung*
4 splendid *prächtig*
5 royal *königlich*
6 highest-ranking *höchstrangig*
7 noble (n, v) *Adlige/r, adlig*
8 servant *Diener/in*
9 crowded *überfüllt*

The palace gardens

The palace had a huge park around it with a new and modern design for its time. There were tens of thousands of trees and hundreds of symmetrical flower beds[1]. A 1.8-km-long canal and many ponds[2] were dug[3] in the gardens. There were also hundreds of statues and fountains[4]. The fountains used so much water that they were turned on all at once only for special events[5]. When the King walked in the gardens, servants would turn on fountains just before he reached them and turn them off after he walked away. All visitors were so fascinated[6] by the gardens that ▸ **monarchs**[7] all over Europe used Versailles as the model for their own palaces. In Germany, for example, palace gardens can still be found today which look like smaller copies of Versailles.

Activate your English

Speaking and writing numbers
a 73-metre-long room
2.76 m (metres) high
60 x (by) 60 cm (centimetres)
8,000 candles
Louis XIV (fourteenth)
one third, two fifths
hundreds of rooms
one per cent

S3 The garden of the Palace of Versailles – then and now

Tasks: The palace and the gardens of Versailles

1 Imagine that you visit the palace and the gardens at Versailles for the first time in 1690. What fascinates you most? Tell your partner.
2 What is most surprising/strange/fascinating about the garden and palace of Versailles … today?
3 List five groups of people who worked in the palace and explain what they did. ***Language help:*** If you don't know the exact word, use the following expressions: *people who worked in … / helped to …*

1 flower bed *Blumenbeet*
2 pond *Teich*
3 to dig, dug, dug *graben*
4 fountain *Springbrunnen*
5 event *Ereignis*
6 to fascinate *faszinieren*
7 monarch *Monarch/in*

S 4 **Sun emblem[1] of Louis XIV on a gate[2] at Versailles**
The sun gives life and warmth, and the planets move around it.

Louis XIV, the Sun King, and his court

Louis XIV called himself the "**Sun King**". He was the centre of all life – in France and in the Palace of Versailles.
There he was surrounded by big groups of people at all times. Only when he visited his wife or mother, or met with ministers did the King really have some private moments.
The **nobles** at his court competed[3] against each other to be near him and to be a part of his daily life. It was an honour for them to be the one who, for example, gave the King his shirt while he was dressing. They felt lucky if they could hold a candle for Louis while he was putting on his wig[4] in the morning. Being so near to the King gave them the respect of other nobles.

Everyday life at court

The King's days – and everybody else's – were organized and planned to the minute: from getting up in the morning and eating, to going to mass and then to bed in the evening. Everybody had to follow strict **rules**. There were exact rules about who could sit next to whom at dinner and who could dance first at a ball.
Of course, **entertainment** played a big role. The best writers and composers[5] worked for the King. Every week there were walks through the garden, hunting, ballets, operas, dancing, plays[6] and concerts. There was also gambling[7] three nights a week where many nobles lost enormous sums of money.
In general, life at court was expensive. If the nobles wanted to be noticed[8] by the King they had to be very fashionable[9]. So they had to buy extremely expensive clothes and wigs. As a result, many nobles were heavily indebted[10] – very often to the King himself.

To be near the King was a must

But although[11] life at Versailles was not easy, the nobles had to spend as much time there as possible. The King just expected[12] them to be near him. Louis made it clear that only those who were close to him counted. Those who did not come to Versailles at all or not often enough could not hope for a job or a favour[13].
But why did the King want the nobles to be around him in his palace?
When Louis was a child, a group of nobles had rebelled against[14] his father and himself. They had threatened to kill them. So he wanted to keep close watch[15] on the nobles. If those who were close to him had many privileges, they would not become rebellious.

1 emblem *Wappen, Abzeichen*
2 gate *Tor*
3 to compete *konkurrieren, wetteifern*
4 wig *Perücke*
5 composer *Komponist/in*
6 play *hier: Drama, Theaterstück*
7 to gamble *um Geld spielen*
8 to notice *bemerken*
9 fashionable *modisch, schick*
10 to be indebted *verschuldet sein*
11 although *obwohl*
12 to expect *erwarten*
13 favour *Gefälligkeit, Gunst*
14 to rebel against sth./sb. *gegen etw./jdn. rebellieren, sich auflehnen*
15 to keep close watch on sb. *jdn. scharf beobachten*

Tasks: Life at Louis XIV's court

1 List key words or phrases to describe life at the Palace of Versailles at the time of Louis XIV (for example: *the palace was crowded*).
2 Discuss if you would have liked to live at the palace. Give reasons why or why not.
3 Identify the ways in which the King controlled the nobles.
4 Give possible reasons why Louis chose the sun as his emblem (**S 4**). What did he want to express with it?

Versailles – the fashion capital of Europe

A noble man's fictional story:

For us **gentlemen** at court, wigs[1] are an absolute must. We don't want to be seen without one. The King was the first to wear one. Rumour has it that[2] he did it to hide the fact that he was bald[3]. But I don't believe it. It makes him look more dignified[4].
Every morning the barber[5] comes to shave my head because then it's easier to wear the wig. The best wigs are made from natural human hair. Cheaper wigs are made of the hair of horses and goats[6], but they look horrible. Nobody I know wears one. Over the wig, a man of style wears a hat decorated with a large feather. Peasants and workers do not wear wigs because they are too expensive and uncomfortable to wear when they are working. They grow their own hair long instead. This lets you know at once who the person is. Their clothes also show it of course because only we nobles are allowed to wear jewels and gold, and only noble men can carry rapiers[7].

A noble lady's fictional story:

We **ladies** (and to be honest all gentlemen too) put on really heavy makeup to make our skin white. Very white skin is the newest fashion here at court. Together with the right rouge for lips and cheeks, it's really attractive. Black beauty patches are also stylish. They are glued to your face when you really want to look good at a ball. My favourite designs are sun, moon and star shapes. They help cover[8] any skin blemishes[9] and the black makes the face even whiter. We don't wash very often. It's just too unhealthy. We use lots of perfume instead. Some say that we do it to cover the bad smell. Well, they may be right.
Our dresses are made of silk in wonderful colours, but only the King and the Queen are allowed to wear gold in their clothes. But at least everybody can use lace[10]. My husband is really angry with me because my last dress cost a fortune[11] since it had so much lace on it. But what can I do? Doesn't he want me to be as well dressed as the Duchess of Condé? And he is following the latest fashion too! Every time the King has something new, he orders something like it at once.
What I absolutely dislike are the hooped skirts underneath the dresses. They make it difficult for women to pass each other in doorways or to sit on sofas. But there's nothing I can do. I won't get invited if I'm not wearing one because noble women are just expected[12] to wear them. Peasant women of course don't wear them because they can't work in them.

S 5 **Hooped skirts (*Reifröcke*) are worn under the dresses, 18th century**

S 6 **Beauty patch, 18th century**

1 wig *Perücke*
2 rumour has it that ... *Gerüchte besagen, dass ...*
3 bald *glatzköpfig*
4 dignified *ehrwürdig*
5 barber *Friseur*
6 goat *Ziege*
7 rapier *Degen*
8 to cover *bedecken*
9 skin blemish *Hautunreinheit*
10 lace *Spitze*
11 fortune *Vermögen*
12 to expect *erwarten*

Tasks: Looking good at the court of Versailles

1 How did noble people dress to show others that they were noble? Make a list.
2 Describe how fashion has changed since the court of Versailles.
3 Do people today also show that they belong to a certain group? If yes, how do they do it? If not, why do they not do it?

6.2 Portrait of a ruler: Portrait of power and wealth

S 7 A royal sceptre

S 8 Portrait of Louis XIV, Hyacinthe Rigaud, Versailles, 1701, oil painting, 2.76 m x (by) 1.94 m

S 9 French *fleur-de-lys*

The painter Rigaud worked for over a year to finish this portrait. It was made as a present for King Philip V of Spain, Louis' grandson. However, Louis and his court liked it so much that he never sent it to Spain.

Looking like a king

At the time when the portrait was painted, Louis was 63 years old. In the painting he is presented in an elegant pose. He is standing with his left hand on his hip. He is looking down at the person in front of the painting. It seems as if a light is shining on Louis, making him brighter than the rest of the painting. It shows every small detail of the King's costume, his wig and even his well-shaped[1] legs with silk[2] stockings[3] and his high-heeled[4] shoes, which he wore because he was not very tall.

The Sun King is wearing the clothes which he was crowned in. His deep blue fur coat[5] is embroidered[6] with the ***fleur-de-lys***, a symbol of France and the French royal family.

The royal sword[7] is at his side, and he is holding the royal sceptre[8]. The crown is on a stool[9] beside him. The throne is behind him on the right and there is an antique column[10] on the left. The colour of the curtain matches the red and gold colours of the carpet[11].

Looking wealthy and powerful

Like other portrait artists of the time the painter Rigaud was not so interested in what the King really looked like, but more interested in making the King look wealthy and powerful. He painted every detail of the work to show the King's greatness.

The fact that Louis XIV kept the portrait and hung it in the throne room at Versailles proves that it showed the way he saw himself and wanted to be seen. People were not allowed to turn their back to the painting and had to act as if the King was actually in front of them and not just a painting.

1 well-shaped *wohl geformt*
2 silk *Seide*
3 stocking *Strumpf*
4 high-heeled *hochhackig*
5 fur coat *Pelzmantel*
6 to embroider *besticken*
7 sword *Schwert*
8 sceptre *Zepter*
9 stool *Schemel*
10 column *Säule*
11 carpet *Teppich*
12 to be surrounded by *umgeben sein von*

Tasks: Analysing a portrait of a ruler

1 Point out how the viewer knows that the person in the painting (**S 8**) is a king.

2 Describe how Rigaud painted the King to look wealthy. ***Language help***: *The painter showed/presented him with/surrounded by*[12] ...

3 Explain why the lighting in the painting is on Louis XIV and not, for example, on the crown and throne.

A costume[1] helped create the king

In 1835, the English author William Thackeray moved to Paris for several years. During his stay in Paris, he visited the Palace of Versailles. There were no kings living there anymore and in 1837, it became a museum. Only some of the paintings and pieces of furniture were still in the palace. Thackeray described his visit in his travel book *Paris Sketch Book*, which was published in 1840. His book also includes the cartoon below.

S 10 **William Thackeray, "*Ludovicus Rex*" (Latin for King Louis), cartoon taken from his *Paris Sketch Book*, London 1840**

S 11 **Thackeray writes about his cartoon:**

You see at once that a king is made out of the wig, the high-heeled shoes and coat, all covered with shiny[2] *fleurs-de-lis*. But there is no king in the small, bald man with the fat stomach[3]. Put the wig and shoes on him, and he is six feet tall; put on the other decorations, and he stands before you like a king and a hero! A king is the work of shoemakers and barbers[4]!

From: William Thackeray, Paris Sketch Book, London 1870, p. 434

Tasks: A costume helped create the King

1 Describe the three figures in the cartoon (**S 10**). Pay special attention to what the King looks like without his stately[5] clothes. Use the text on p. 78 for help.
2 Analyse the cartoon with the help of the History skills on p. 64.
3 Explain what Thackeray wants to express with his statement "A king is the work of shoemakers and barbers!"
4 Today the Palace of Versailles is one of the biggest tourist attractions in France. Go to the museum's homepage http://en.chateauversailles.fr/ and plan a visit to the palace.

1 costume *Kostüm*
2 shiny *glänzend*
3 stomach *Bauch*
4 barber *Friseur*
5 stately *herschaftlich*

6.3 I am the state and no one is my equal

S 12 The caption in French says: "The King in his Council[1]. He decides on war or peace." Print, 1682.

It shows the King, his brother and the crown prince together with the ministers.

Louis' system of government

Louis XIV became king at the age of five when his father, Louis XIII, died. But Louis only truly controlled the government at the age of twenty-three after the death of his prime minister[2] in 1661. At that time he decided to be a real king and to govern[3] himself.

S 13 Louis XIV told his ministers

It is now time that I govern ... myself. You [secretaries and ministers of state] will help me with your advice when I ask for it. I order you to seal no orders[4] except by my command ... I order you not to sign anything, not even a passport ... without my command; to report to me personally each day and to favour[5] no one.

From: Geoffrey Treasure, The making of modern Europe, 1648-1780, London 1985, p. 249

Historians believe that Louis XIV also told his ministers: "**I am the state**". This meant that only he had a say[6] in how France was governed. He did not have to share the power[7] to govern France with anybody else. Only his word was the law. He could send people to prison with just one letter. No explanations and no trial[8] were necessary. He decided on war, peace and taxes.

Louis XIV governed with **ministers and secretaries of state**, who he met with four times a week. He usually appointed[9] non-nobles as ministers. Before 1661, these ministers were nobles. The ministers had the right to advise the king, but he always made the last decision. He also appointed **governors**[10]. They were sent to the different French provinces to collect taxes, oversee[11] trials, and make sure[12] that all royal laws were obeyed. They had to inform the King about anything that happened there. The King did not tolerate any resistance[13].

This was completely different from how France was ruled before. Before 1661, powerful nobles had the power in the French provinces and often rebelled against the kings. The last time they tried to do that was when Louis was a child, and his life was in great danger.

Key term

Absolutism and the theory of the "divine right[14] of Kings"

The form of government where the ▸ **monarch's**[15] power was complete or absolute was called "**absolutism**" or "**absolute monarchy**" and the monarch was called an "**absolute monarch**". His or her power was not limited[16]. No other people had a say on how the country was governed.

People believed that God chose the monarchs and gave them the right to rule. This is called the "**divine right of Kings**". This theory said that monarchs were God's representatives[17] on earth. The monarchs were only responsible to God for what they did or did not do. Consequently, they stood above everybody else. Everybody had to obey their orders. Those who criticized them were also criticizing God.

1 King's Council *Ratgeber des Königs, Kabinett*
2 prime minister *Ministerpräsident/in, Premieminister/in*
3 to govern *regieren*
4 to seal an order *die Gültigkeit eines Befehls mit einem Siegel bestätigen (besiegeln)*
5 to favour *bevorzugen*
6 to have a say in sth. *bei etw. Mitspracherecht haben*
7 power *Macht, Gewalt*
8 trial *Gerichtsverfahren*
9 to appoint *ernennen*
10 governor *a person who governs for the king*
11 to oversee sth. *etw. überwachen*
12 to make sure *sicherstellen*
13 resistance *Widerstand*
14 divine right *Gottesgnadentum*
15 monarch *Monarch/in*
16 to limit sth. *etw. beschränken, begrenzen*
17 representative *Vertreter/in, Abgeordnete/r*

France dominated Europe

France dominated[1] Europe politically and culturally at the end of the 17th and during the18th century. It had the strongest and best organized army on the European continent with 100,000 to 160,000 soldiers. In different wars, France won new areas in the north and east. Its only rival[2] was Great Britain because the Holy Roman Empire was weak after the Thirty Years' War.
Culturally, France was the trendsetter in Europe and many aspects of French life were copied. Princes everywhere built palaces like Versailles and filled them with splendid French furniture and paintings. Learned[3] people and the nobles at the courts in Europe not only spoke and wrote in French, but they also dressed and danced like the French.

S 14 French loan words[4] in German

German has borrowed many words from French. They show which aspects of French life were new to Germans. Many of the French loan words in German also look like English words because English has borrowed them too.
Kommandant, schick, Ball, Nische, Patrouille, amüsieren, Minister, charmant, Ballett, Fassade, Parfum, Uniform, Portion, Dessert, Kaserne, Friseur, Kabinett, Kostüm, rasieren, Präsident, Perücke, Kotelett, Etage, Kommode, Leutnant, Dekoration, Vitrine, Balkon, Pistole, Kavalier

S 15 Judging[5] absolutism

An unknown author published[6] the novel[7] "The adventures of Telemachus" in 1699. It became one of the most popular books in the 18th century. The author said:
Rulers that have become used[8] to regarding their will as law may do anything. They govern without principle[9]. They are flattered[10] and feared everywhere; their subjects[11] degenerate[12] into slaves. Nobody dares[13] to tell them the truth[14]. Some sudden[15] and violent[16] revolution[17] only can limit this enormous power ...

From: François de Salignac de La Mothe-Fénelon, The adventures of Telemachus, vol.1, p. 387

Tasks: Louis XIV and the rule of an absolute monarch

1 Compare how the artist presented the king and his ministers in **S 12**. Do we know who is who?

2 Say in your own words what the king told his ministers in **S 13**.
Language help: *He forbade ... /didn't let/allow... to.*

3 Read the text on p. 80. Very often Louis' system of government is presented in a diagram[18] like the one on the right. Copy and label[19] it.

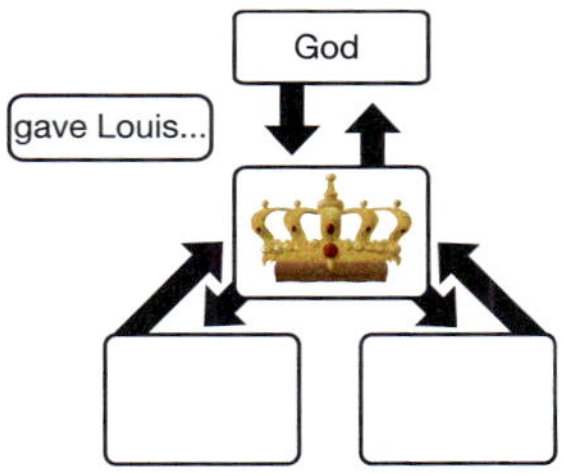

4 "Absolute monarchs can do what they want." True or false? Give reasons.

5 **a** List the author's complaints about absolute rulers (**S 15**).
b The author writes that only a violent revolution can limit the rule of an absolute monarch. Give possible reasons why he thinks so.

6 French loan words in German: parts of buildings, noble lifestyle and ... (see **S 14**). Copy the table; find more headings and fill in. In which word fields did the German language borrow most from? What does that prove?

Parts of buildings	...	***Noble lifestyle***	...	...	...
Etage	*Präsident*		*Kotelett*		
...					

1 to dominate *vorherrschen, dominieren*
2 rival *Rivale/Rivalin*
3 learned *gebildet*
4 loan word *Lehnwort*
5 to judge sth. *etw. beurteilen*
6 to publish *veröffentlichen*
7 novel *Roman*
8 to become used to sth. *sich an etw. gewöhnen*
9 principle *Prinzip*
10 to flatter *schmeicheln*
11 subject *hier: Untertan/in*
12 to degenerate *sich zurückentwickeln*
13 to dare sth. *etw. wagen*
14 truth *Wahrheit*
15 sudden *plötzlich*
16 violent *gewaltsam*
17 revolution = the changing of a government of a country by violent action
18 diagram *schematische Darstellung, Diagramm*
19 to label *beschriften*

6.4 New industries for the King

S 16 Jean-Baptiste Colbert, painting by Claude Lefebvre, 1660

Colbert wanted to create new industries and make trade grow

Louis XIV spent enormous sums of money on the court and the army, as well as to build and decorate his palaces. However, state income[1] (the taxes) was never high enough to pay for all of it. As a result the King spent more than he had and his debts[2] grew. But the King did not want to save money. Therefore the new **Minister of Finances ▸ Jean-Baptiste Colbert** (1619–1683) had to find ways to increase[3] state income. To make people pay higher taxes seemed impossible. Most of the French were poor peasants who could not pay more. And to make the nobles and the Church (the bishops and abbots) pay taxes was impossible if the King did not want to risk a rebellion.

Since Colbert could not increase the taxes, he did something completely different to increase state income: he took measures[4] to help start new industries in France and to make French trade grow. He knew that the King and the nobles bought big amounts of fabrics[5], tapestries[6], mirrors, lace[7] and silk from other countries each year. Could these goods not be produced in France? More French people would have a job, the owners of the industries would make a profit – and the French state would get higher taxes from more people.

S 17 The founding[8] of the Royal Glass and Mirror Company[9] in Paris

Mirrors were rare[10] and an absolute luxury in the 17th century. They cost[11] more than a painting. In 1650 the biggest mirror in France was sixty by sixty centimetres. The glassmakers in the Republic of Venice in Italy were the only ones in Europe who could produce perfect mirrors. When it became fashionable to decorate the rooms with mirrors to make them brighter, the French King and his nobles ordered hundreds of mirrors from Venice. Enormous sums of money were paid to Venetian[12] glassmakers each year.

In 1665 Colbert founded the Royal Glass and Mirror Company and ordered the French ambassador[13] to go to Venice. There he had to secretly find Venetian glassmakers who were willing to come to Paris and teach French workers the secret of making perfect mirrors. To find these men was not easy because the glassmakers were strictly forbidden to leave Venice. But the French ambassador offered them even more money. With some tricks, he convinced around 20 men to leave Venice. The Venetian ambassador in Paris then tried everything to stop them from giving the French the glass and mirror-making secrets and make them go back to Venice. However most of them stayed and the production of glass and mirrors soon started.

The company's success began when the King ordered the first mirrors for his future Hall of Mirrors in the Palace of Versailles. The company still exists today.

From: Joan DeJean, The Essence of Style, New York, 2005, p.177 ff.

1 state income *Staatseinkommen*
2 debts *Schulden*
3 to increase sth./increase (v, n) *etw. erhöhen / Erhöhung*
4 to take measures *Maßnahmen ergreifen*
5 fabric *Stoff, Tuch*
6 tapestry *Wandteppich*
7 lace *Spitze*
8 to found *gründen*
9 company *Firma, Unternehmen*
10 rare *selten, rar*
11 to cost, cost, cost *kosten*
12 Venetian *venezianisch*
13 ambassador *Botschafter/in*

Tasks: Producing mirrors in France (S 17)

1 "Glassmakers are not allowed to leave Venice." You are a member of the Venice city government. Explain why you made it illegal. ***Language help:*** *If the workers leave Venice ...*

2 You, as the Venetian ambassador, want to tell Colbert that he used unacceptable and criminal methods to start a new industry in France. Write down your arguments.

3 You are Colbert's secretary. Write a letter in which you defend Colbert's measures.

Were Colbert's measures a success[1] or failure[2]?

S 18 Creating new industries and making trade grow: Colbert's letter to the town officials[3] and people of Marseille in 1664

Marseille was the second biggest French port and situated[4] at the mouth[5] of the river Rhone on the Mediterranean Sea (*Mittelmeer*).

We also inform you:
That we are going to pay big sums of money for the trading companies[6] of the West Indies and East Indies [today Malaysia and Indonesia];
That we are working constantly to abolish[7] all the tolls[8] which the ships have to pay on the rivers;
That more than a million livres[9] have already been paid for the repair of the roads;
That we will help all those who wish to re-establish[10] old industries or to establish new ones by giving them money;
That all the sea merchants who buy ships, or who build new ones, will get money from us.

From: http://www.mtholyoke.edu/acad/intrel/colbert.htm

First, Colbert was quite successful. The **new trading companies** imported more and more expensive raw materials[11] like sugar, tobacco and spices from the **French colonies** in the Americas and Asia. The new industries with their specialist workers produced finished goods[12] like mirrors or fine fabrics[13], for example. The workers were forbidden to leave the country on pain of death[14].

Colbert then put high ▸ **customs duties**[15] on imports of finished goods, which were also produced in France. Because of this, the mirrors made in Venice, for example, became more expensive in France than the French mirrors. As a result, the French now bought more goods made in France. But people outside of France also wanted the new fashionable French goods, so the exports[16] of French goods to other countries increased. Therefore French industries grew and more people worked there. This meant that the owners and workers of the new industries in France were paying more taxes and French state income went up.

However, Louis XIV did not stop the wars between France and its neighbours, so at the end of the King's life, France was nearly bankrupt[17]. Another negative aspect was that other countries were also now starting to do what France had done earlier: founding new industries and then putting high customs duties on imported goods, like from France.

Tasks: Colbert's measures

1 Colbert's letter (**S 18**). Copy and finish the sentences.
- a The French government paid money
  - to companies which traded with the East and West Indies because …
  - to persons who wanted to start old industries again and found new ones because …
  - for road repairs because …
  - to merchants who bought ships because …
- b The French government worked to abolish tolls on the rivers because …

2 Point out what happened when, for example, the government of the Netherlands
- a put customs duties on the goods which were imported from France
- b helped found a mirror industry in the Netherlands.

3 Give possible reasons why Colbert's measures were a success or failure. ***Language help:*** *on the one hand …. On the other hand …*

1 success *Erfolg*
2 failure *Misserfolg, Versagen*
3 official *Amtsperson, Beamter/Beamtin*
4 to be situated *gelegen sein*
5 mouth *hier: Mündung*
6 trading company *Handelsgesellschaft*
7 to abolish *abschaffen*
8 toll *Mautgebühren*
9 livres *französische Währung im 17. Jh.*
10 to re-establish *neu einrichten*
11 raw material *Rohstoff*
12 finished goods *Fertigwaren*
13 fabric *Stoff, Tuch*
14 on pain of death *unter Androhung der Todesstrafe*
15 customs duties *Zollgebühren*
16 export (n) / to export (v) *Ausfuhr, Export / ausführen, exportieren*
17 bankrupt *bankrott, pleite*

6.5 Louis's subjects

In 1660 the French population was 17 million, which was around one fifth of the whole European population. Spain and England each had a population of only 5 million.
The population in France, as in the rest of Europe, was divided into **three estates**[1].

Key term

What was an estate?
An estate was a very large group of people. Each group had different rights. The highest was the clergy[2] (priests, monks), then came the nobility[3] (the noble lords) and the lowest were the working people. People's birth decided which estate they belonged to (second and third estate). The first and second estates had many privileges[4].

The First Estate was the clergy (2 % [= per cent] of the population). About 30 % of the land in France belonged to the Church. Bishops and abbots (most often the sons of noble families) had enormous incomes; priests in the villages, however, earned much less. The clergy collected fees[5] and tithes[6] (10 % of everything which the peasants produced).

The Second Estate was the nobility (1 % of the population). They owned 40 % of the land. Although they had lost their powers to govern in France, they still had many privileges. They did not have to pay taxes and the peasants had to pay dues to them. They got the well-paid jobs in the army and at the court of Versailles. They were the only ones who were allowed to hunt[7]. Although some were extremely wealthy, many noblemen were not very rich and had to work on their land. Many had debts because their lifestyles were expensive.

The Third Estate was everybody else (97 % of the population). Some were servants, craftsmen[8], shopkeepers[9], doctors and seamen, but more than 80 % of the third estate were poor peasants. They had to pay fees, dues[10] and tithes to the first and second estate in addition to[11] the royal taxes.
However, some people of the Third Estate became extremely rich as merchants, bankers or ship owners. Then they often bought noble titles, like Colbert for example, who belonged to the Third Estate as a son of a merchant family, but who died as a noble count[12].

1 estate *Stand*
2 clergy *Geistlichkeit, Klerus*
3 nobility *Adel*
4 privilege *Privileg, Sonderrecht*
5 fee *Gebühr*
6 tithe *der (Kirchen-) Zehnte, Kirchensteuer*
7 to be allowed to hunt *das Jagdrecht besitzen*
8 craftsman *Handwerker/in*
9 shopkeeper *Ladeninhaber/in*
10 dues *Abgaben (in Form von Geld, Waren oder Dienstleistungen)*
11 in addition to *zusätzlich*
12 count *Graf*
13 society *Gesellschaft*

Tasks: The three estates

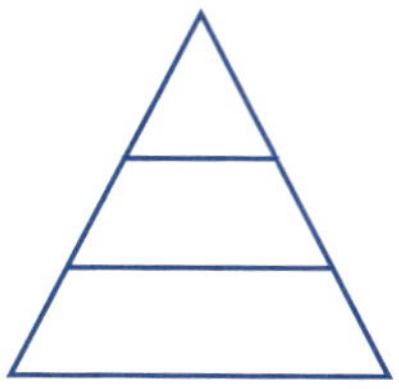

1 Very often the three estates of French society[13] in the 17th century are shown in a pyramid like the one on the left. Copy and label it. Before you begin, think of the following questions: Who is above the pyramid/at the top/at the bottom? Should the pyramid be divided in the same way as in the example to the left?
2 Many people in the third estate were very angry at the privileges of the First and Second Estate. Discuss which one they were most angry at.
3 Explain why wealthy people of the third estate tried to become noble.

Unit revision

Louis XIV and the Age of Absolutism

Activate your English

Speaking and writing numbers

Key personalities

Louis XIV • Colbert

Key terms

Absolutism • absolute monarch • Hall of Mirrors • Palace of Versailles • estate • divine right of kings

History skills

Creating diagrams • analysing a portrait of a ruler

S 19 A peasant who lived near Versailles, ca. 1780

S 20 A noble couple at the Palace of Versailles, 18th century

Revision tasks: Louis XIV and the Age of Absolutism

1 Imagine you are a visitor travelling through France in 1690. You ask different people what they think of their life. Write down what they say and present it in class.

2 Tell your partner what rights Louis XIV had and give possible reasons why he did not have any nobles as ministers.

3 Explain why the author of *Telemachus* (**S 15**) did not want to publish his name at first.

4 Very often a diagram like the one in **S 21** is used to present Colbert's measures to increase French state income. Make a key for the different symbols (for example, ——— "roads are repaired").

5 Write these phrases in English:
ein 1,8 km langer Kanal
Ludwig war 1, 64 m groß.
drei Viertel der Franzosen
hunderte von Besuchern
97 Prozent der Franzosen

S 21 Colbert's measures in France 1665–1683

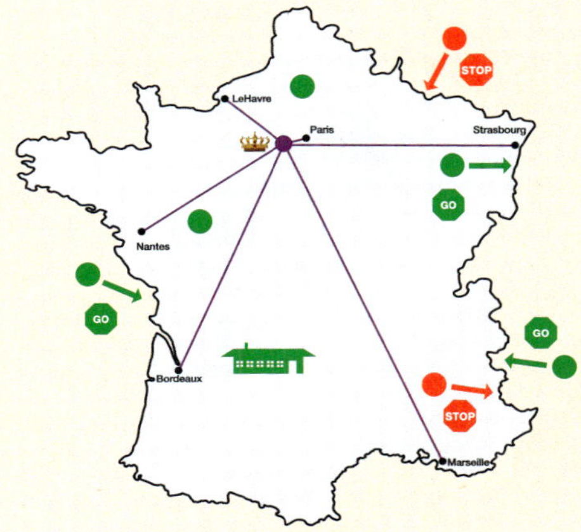

Glossary of terms and persons

Absolutism: see Key term, *p. 80*

AD and BC: see Key term, *p. 7*

Age of Discovery: this period started in the 15th century, when Europeans began to explore Africa, Asia and ▶ the Americas. *p. 51*

America – the Americas: see Key term, *p. 51*

Aztec Empire: the Aztecs were a people in Central Mexico. They formed the Aztec Empire, an alliance of three city-states that ruled large parts of Mexico from 1428 until the Spanish conquerors and native allies (Verbündete) under ▶ Cortés defeated them in 1521. *p. 54*

book illumination: in the Middle Ages, all books were handwritten originals. The images in the handwritten texts are called "illuminations" because they were often made in gold, silver, etc. (illuminare = the Latin word for "to light up"). *p. 15*

Byzantine Empire: see Key term, *p. 33*

chronicle: comes from the Greek word for "time" and is a written account of historical events and facts in a chronological order (meaning the events are described in the order in which they happened). *p. 36*

(the) Church: see Key term, *p. 21*

Church of the Holy Sepulchre: is a church in the city of Jerusalem. It is built upon the place where Jesus was crucified (nailed to the cross), buried, and resurrected (raised from the dead). The church is an important pilgrimage destination for Christians. *p. 36*

Colbert, Jean-Baptiste (1619–1683): was the French Minister of Finances under King ▶ Louis XIV. While the king was spending a lot of money on wars and his palace, Colbert was trying to rescue the French economy. He established new industries in France, for example, the Royal Glass and Mirror Company, so that products did not have to be imported any more (which was very expensive). *p. 82*

Columbus, Christopher (1451 – 1506): was an Italian explorer. Under the Spanish crown, he went on four voyages across the Atlantic Ocean. He was looking for a new trading route to the ▶ East Indies. Instead, he discovered ▶ the Americas and began the Spanish colonization of the ▶ New World, while also spreading Christianity. *p. 50*

Cortés, Hernán (1485–1547): was a Spanish colonizer. He led an expedition to Mexico, which caused the fall of the ▶ Aztec Empire. *p. 54*

Copernicus, Nicolaus (1473–1543): was an astronomer in ▶ Renaissance times and the first scientist who proved that the Earth is not the centre of the solar system. He came up with the ▶ heliocentric model, placing the sun in the centre of the solar system, which went against the Church's worldview. p. 46

Crusades: see Key term, *p. 33*

customs duties: the money that must be paid at the border of a country if you want to import goods from other countries; this makes imported goods more expensive. *p. 83*

da Gama, Vasco (1460 or 1469–1524): was a Portuguese explorer during the ▶ Age of Discovery. He was the first European to reach India over the sea, which made it possible for Portugal to build up a long lasting colonial empire in Asia and to make its economy better through the spice trade. *p. 53*

da Vinci, Leonardo (1452–1519): was an Italian with many talents: he was a painter, sculptor, architect, scientist, mathematician, inventor, anatomist, map maker, musician and writer. He is seen as a genius and said to represent the ideals of the ▶ Renaissance. *p. 45*

de Sahagún, Bernhardino (1499–1590): was a Spanish missionary priest who travelled to New Spain (today's Mexico) and spent more than 50 years on his missionary task there. During that time, he also studied and wrote about ▶ Aztec beliefs, culture, history and language, and gave an insight into the worldview and culture of Aztec people. *p. 54*

Diaz, Bartolomeo (ca. 1450–1500): was a Portuguese explorer and the first European to sail around the southern tip of Africa. The King of Portugal gave him the task of finding a trading route to India. *p. 52*

divine right of kings: means that a king is ruled by no one on earth, and only by God. The king's right to rule is God's will. Because of this, the king does not have to listen to his people, the aristocracy, or even the Church. Even if the king is unfair, only God can judge him and if the king is overthrown, it would be going against what God wants (*Gottesgnadentum*). *p. 80*

East & West Indies: "East Indies" is what Europeans have called south and southeastern Asia since the 16th century, while "West Indies" refers to the Caribbean (*Karibik*). *p. 53*

estate: see Key term, *p. 64*

excommunication – to excommunicate: the Church can excommunicate members if they have broken the Church's rules or if they have a different opinion than the Church. This person is excluded from the religious community until he or she stops or corrects the wrong behaviour. *p. 60*

Galen, Claudius (129–ca. 200): was a well-known Roman physician (*Arzt*) and philosopher. His research influenced science for hundreds of years, especially in the fields of medicine. His theories on human anatomy (developed through the dissection of pigs and monkeys) were not questioned until the middle of the 16th century (see also ▶ Vesalius), and his writings were still studied by medical students in the 19th century. *p. 48*

Galilei, Galileo (1564–1642): was an Italian astronomer, mathematician, doctor and philosopher whose work was very important for the Scientific Revolution (*Wissenschaftliche Revolution*). His theories in astronomy and his support for ▶ Copernicus's ▶ heliocentric model of the solar system made him a ▶ heretic in the eyes of the Church. The Church forced him to live under house arrest for the rest of his life. However, he wrote one of his most brilliant works during that time, which summarised his studies. *p. 46*

geocentric theory: see "heliocentric model of the solar system".

German kings and emperors: In 936 representatives of all the German tribes elected Otto I to be the first King of Germany. He was crowned in Aachen Cathedral on the throne of Charlemagne (Karl der Große) (see photo on page 6). Twenty-six years later in 962, Otto I was crowned emperor of the Holy Roman Empire of the German Nation by Pope John XII in Rome. Eight centuries of Holy Roman emperors followed. Beginning in 1356, the emperors were elected by seven powerful German rulers. Between 1493 and 1806, all of the emperors except for one were members of the Habsburg family. The Habsburg family were the rulers in Austria, as well as in several other areas. In 1806, the Holy Roman Empire of the German Nation came to an end when the last Holy Roman Emperor, Francis II abdicated his throne (*abdanken*). *p. 12*

Gutenberg, Johannes (ca. 1398–1468): invented printing. Before that, books and texts had to be copied by hand, which took a long time. His invention of a machine that could print texts fast and easily is seen as one of the most important events in history. Among other things, it played a key role in the ▶ Renaissance, ▶ the Protestant Reformation, and the Age of Enlightenment (*Aufklärung*). *p. 63*

heliocentric model of the solar system: until ▶ Copernicus presented proof for this model, people believed that earth was the centre of the solar system and that the sun and other planets moved around it (= geocentric model). But he showed in his work that it was the other way around: the sun is in the centre of the solar system and earth moves around it. ▶ Galileo supported this theory. *p. 46*

heretic: see Key term, *p. 47*

Holy Communion: is the Christian act of eating bread and drinking wine to remember Jesus, who, as it is told in the Bible, said to his followers during the Last Supper (*Abendmahl*) that the food and drink were his body and his blood. *p. 19*

(the) Holy Land: see Key term, *p. 33*

(the) Incas: the Inca civilization arose in the 13th century, with their political centre in today's Peru (South America). The Inca Empire was the largest empire in America before the time of ▶ Columbus's discovery. *p. 54*

kings and emperors: see "German kings and emperors"

letters of indulgence: in the ▶ Middle Ages, people thought that they would have to go to purgatory (*Fegefeuer*) after their death for all the bad things (sins) they had done in life. But the Church told them that if they bought letters of indulgence, their time in purgatory would become shorter. In reality, the Church needed the money for many reasons (for example, to build new churches and to pay for the crusades). *p. 60*

lord and lady: a lord was a powerful man in Europe during the Middle Ages, often a knight. Usually, he owned a lot of land and property. The wives and daughters of lords are called ladies. Lords and ladies belonged to the nobility. *p. 9*

Louis XIV (dt. *Ludwig XIV.*, 1638–1715): was the king of France for a very long period of time: over 72 years. He is also called the "Sun King". He made himself an absolute monarch, which meant that he ruled France alone, and he believed that his power came from God. Because he did not like Paris, he moved the government from Paris to Versailles. He had the nobility on his side and became one of the most powerful monarchs, supporting the ideals of ▶ Absolutism. *p.74*

Luther, Martin (1483–1546): was a German monk, priest and professor of theology, and was a key figure in the ▶ Protestant Reformation. He did not agree with the idea that people could free themselves from God's punishment for their sins by buying ▶ letters of indulgence. In his opinion, God would forgive those who believed in Jesus Christ. Therefore he wrote his 95 Theses in 1517. When he did not say he was wrong, Luther was ▶ excommunicated from the Church and made an outlaw. During his exile at ▶ Wartburg, he translated the Bible from Latin into German, so that everyone could understand it. This not only had an enormous influence on the Church, but also on the German language (which now had a common point of reference for a standard form). *p. 60*

Mecca: is a city in Saudi Arabia. As the birthplace of ▶ Mohammed, it is the holiest city in the religion of Islam. Millions of pilgrims go there every year because all Muslims must go on a pilgrimage to Mecca once in their life if they are able to do so. *p. 30*

Middle Ages: see Key term, *p. 7*

Mohammed (ca. 570–632): was a religious leader from ▶ Mecca who united Arabia under Islam. Muslims believe he is a messenger (*Bote*) and prophet of God. *p. 30*

monarch: is a person at the head of a ▶ monarchy (for example, a king or queen), who rules a country. A monarch normally takes over the throne after the death of his/her parents, who are also monarchs, and then rules his/her whole life. *p. 75, 80*

monarchy: is a form of government. It means that a state is ruled or controlled by a single person. *p. 75, 80*

Native Americans: see Key term, *p. 53*

(the) New World: when ▶ the Americas were discovered in the ▶ Middle Ages, people called the land "the New World". Before that, everyone thought that there was only Europe, Asia and Africa. *p. 53*

Noble men and women: see Key term, *p. 13*

Pope Urban II (1042–1099): was pope from 1088 until his death in 1099. He is best known for beginning the First Crusade (1096 –1099). He promised that God would forgive all the sins of those who died during the crusade. This gave many people a reason to fight in the battles. *p. 32*

Prince Henry (1394–1460): is also called Prince Henry the Navigator from Portugal. He wanted to know if one could sail around Africa to reach India, and paid captains and map makers to explore the African coast. *p. 52*

Protestant Reformation: when ▶ Luther posted his 95 Theses, many people agreed with his critical arguments. He and his supporters were against (= they protested) the structure, the rules and the rituals of the Catholic Church. This led to the creation of Protestant churches all over the country and to the formation of a new group within Christianity called "Protestantism". *p 60, 67*

race: The word "race" was used in the past to describe a large group of people who came from the same place, spoke the same language and looked the same. Today, we speak of population (*Bevölkerung*) or ethnic group (*Volksgruppe*). *p. 32*

Ramadan (fast): is a Muslim holiday, which takes place in the ninth month of the Islamic calendar. During the holiday, adult Muslims must fast. This means that they are not allowed to eat, drink or smoke from sunrise to sunset. *p. 36*

Renaissance: a period or cultural movement from the 14th to the 17th century that started in Italy and soon spread all over Europe. It influenced the whole intellectual life at that time, especially literature, philosophy, art, music, politics, science and religion. *p. 44*

Roman Empire: was a very large empire, which stretched from Britain and Germany to North Africa and the Persian Gulf at the time of its greatest power. It was founded in 27 BC and lasted until 476 AD. In 395, the empire was split into two: the ▸ Byzantine Empire and the Western Roman Empire. Some of the influences of the Roman Empire were straight roads, calendars, many important laws, and a basis for many languages.

Shrine of the Three Kings: the bones of the Three Kings (= the Biblical Magi) are said to be inside this large golden sarcophagus (*Steinsarg*). It is found in ▸ the Cologne Cathedral (*Kölner Dom*) and attracts many pilgrims. German: *Dreikönigsschrein. p. 30*

smallpox: is an infectious (*ansteckend*) disease that only affects humans. It is believed to have existed since 10,000 BC. There are different types, which show different kinds of pustules or bumps all over the skin. Some types cause many patients to die; the more serious type has a death rate of 30–35%. The disease was responsible for about 300–500 million deaths just during the 20th century, but vaccination campaigns (*Impfkampagnen*) put an end to the disease in 1979. *p. 56*

source: a book, statement, letter, chronicle, painting, radio, ..., video, etc. which gives information about an event, especially from the past. *p. 36*

St. Peter's Basilica (Papal Basilica of Saint Peter): is situated in Vatican City and is one of the most important churches in Christianity. Its construction took more than one hundred years: from 1506 to 1626. The basilica is where Saint Peter, one of Jesus' twelve apostles, is buried. It is not only one of the largest churches in the world, but also an extraordinary piece of art (Michelangelo worked there). It is seen as the greatest building of its age. *p. 60*

Thirty Year's War: was a series of wars that took place over a long period of time (ca. 1618 – 1648). It started as a conflict between Catholics and Protestants in the ▸ Holy Roman Empire, but fights over the power within the Empire played an important role too. These long periods of war brought hunger and destruction to the people. *p. 68*

Tithe: one tenth ($=\frac{1}{10}$) of the goods or agricultural products that someone produced, or one tenth of the money they earned, which had to be paid as a tax to the Church. *p. 21, 84*

Toscanelli, Paolo (1397–1482): was an Italian mathematician, astronomer and mapmaker. He had the idea that ships from Europe could reach Asia if they went west across the Atlantic Ocean. ▸ Columbus believed him and wanted to prove that Toscanelli was correct. *p. 50*

Triangular Trade: This trade connected Europe, Africa and the Americas across the Atlantic. For over 350 years, merchants shipped goods from Europe to Africa, sold them there, and bought slaves. They took the slaves to the Americas and then charged their ships with different goods (for example tobacco) and brought those back to Europe. This meant wealth for the port cities and merchants, but also suffering for the numerous slaves, who came to the Americas against their will to work on the plantations. *p. 57*

Vesalius, Andreas (1514–1564): was a Flemish anatomist and doctor. He wrote one of the most important works on human anatomy called *On the structure of the Human Body*. Vesalius learned that ▸ the famous physician Claudius Galen had gained his knowledge by dissecting animals. Vesalius corrected Galen's work by dissecting human bodies. He is also called the founder of modern human anatomy. *p. 48*

Vespucci, Amerigo (ca. 1454–1512): was an Italian explorer, navigator and mapmaker. He was the first to understand that the land which was discovered by ▸ Columbus was not the eastern border of Asia, but a new continent. *p. 53*

villein (also villain): villeins normally rented houses and land from their landlords. The villeins not only worked on their own land, but also had to help in the fields of their landlord (especially during the harvest-time). But most of the time, they could work on their own land. Villeins were not free to live wherever they wanted: they needed the agreement of their lord to move away. *p. 14*

West Indies: see "East & West Indies".

World Heritage site: is a place that is on a list by UNESCO (United Nations Educational, Scientific and Cultural Organization) for its special cultural or physical importance. World Heritage sites can be for example mountains, forests, buildings, monuments, or whole cities. Today there are over 900 sites found in the list, which are spread all over the world. You can find a list of the World Heritage sites mentioned in this book on *p. 89.*

UNESCO World Heritage sites

Aachen Cathedral: Aachen Cathedral is also known as the Imperial Cathedral. It is a Roman Catholic church, located in Aachen, Germany. In 792, Emperor Charlemagne began building the church and today, it is the oldest cathedral in northern Europe. From 936 to 1531, thirty German kings and twelve German queens were crowned in the church. There are several very important religious objects in the church which were collected by Charlemagne during his lifetime. Two of these objects are the blankets which were believed to be wrapped around Jesus Christ as a baby and a piece of the Virgin Mary's clothing. They are shown every seven years for pilgrims who come to visit. Many Christians have made pilgrimages to the historical Aachen Cathedral. Some other interesting things to see at the church are Charlemagne's throne and the shrine which holds his bones. *p. 6*

Cerro Rico: see "Potosí".

Cologne Cathedral: The building of the Cologne Cathedral began in 1248 and ended six centuries later, in 1880. During that time, the construction was started and stopped several times because there was sometimes not enough money and also not enough interest to continue. In 1848, construction began again on the cathedral and it was finally finished 32 years later. During World War II, the cathedral was bombed and very badly damaged, but luckily could be rebuilt. Today, over 80 specialists work on the building to keep it in good condition and fight problems which are caused by weather and the environment. The cathedral is large enough for 20,000 people. Among its eight bells, there is St. Peter's Bell, which weighs 21,772 kilograms and is the largest freely swinging church bell in the world. Visitors can see it as they climb the 533 steps to the platform on the cathedral's south tower. *p. 30*

Elmina Castle: Elmina Castle was built by the Portuguese in 1482, and today it is the oldest European building south of the Sahara. It was originally built as a trading post to protect the traded gold, but later it became an important place to stop in the Atlantic slave trade. The Atlantic slave trade took place between the 16th and 19th centuries and involved the buying and selling of African men and women into slavery. Elmina Castle was used as a place to trade these humans, brought by African kings and chiefs to trade in exchange for textiles and horses. Slaves, who had been bought by the Portuguese, waited in a small area where there was not even enough room to lie down and nowhere to use the bathroom. Then, ships carried them off to Brazil and other Portuguese colonies to work. In 1637, the Dutch took over the castle and continued to use the building to help in their slave trading. Then, in 1872, the British Empire took over the Dutch Gold Coast and the fort. *p. 57*

Hanseatic City of Lübeck: Lübeck was at one time the capital of the Hanseatic League, a northern European trade organization from the 12th to the 16th centuries. Because it was the major trading centre in Northern Europe, the city and many of its people were very rich. In 1226, Emperor Frederick II said that Lübeck was an Imperial Free City, which meant that it had no other ruler except the emperor. As an Imperial Free City, they had a lot of power. They could go to war or make peace as they wished, and they could make a lot of their own decisions through the city council. Although the city was damaged during the Second World War, the basic construction of the city is still the same as it was in the 15th and 16th centuries. Today, there are about 214,000 inhabitants. The houses of Thomas Mann, Willy Brandt, and Günther Grass can be found in Lübeck. The city is also famous for its marzipan, a paste made of almonds, sugar and egg whites, often covered in chocolate. *p. 6*

Historic Centre of Rome: Modern historians believe that Rome was founded in 625 BC. Because of its long history, some people even call it the "Eternal City". Rome was first a kingdom, ruled by kings for over 200 years. Then, it was a Republic for about 500 years and after that, it was an Empire for another 500 years. Many important ideas came from Rome, like the calendar, the basis for several languages, many important architectural designs, and political ideas, like democracy. Since the 4th century, Rome has also been the capital of the Christian world, and today the headquarters of the Catholic Church are located in Vatican City in Rome. Nowadays, there are still many monuments and ruins in existence which can be visited. One important historical monument is the Colosseum, which took eight years to build (72 AD to 80 AD) and was the largest amphitheatre in the Roman Empire. 45,000 people could sit and watch the bloody battles, which took place between gladiators, or sometimes humans against animals. Another interesting site is the Pantheon, which was first built in 27 AD, then rebuilt in 126 AD, and was a temple to all of the gods.

Istanbul: Istanbul is the largest city in Turkey and has a very long history, beginning over 2,500 years ago. The city is also the only one in the world which is on two separate continents: Asia and Europe. It was originally called Constantinople and it was the capital of the ▸ Byzantine Empire. The Byzantine Empire began in 395 AD when the Roman Empire was divided. Although the western part became weaker, the Byzantine Empire remained strong. From 500 AD to 1200 AD, Constantinople was the richest city in Europe and Asia. Today there are still many interesting places to visit, which show the long history of the place and its importance to arts, politics and culture. One of them is the Hippodrome of Constantinople, which was a place for sporting events and horse racing. Another is the Basilica Cistern, which was an underground well, built by the Byzantine Emperor Justinian in 532 AD to provide freshwater for people living in Constantinople. While walking through the cistern, fish can be seen swimming under the walkways. *p. 33*

Jerusalem: see "Old City of Jerusalem and its Walls".

Krak des Chevaliers: Krak des Chevaliers ("Fortress of Knights") is one of the most important existing castles from the ▸ Middle Ages. This Crusader castle can be found in Syria and looks almost the same as it did during the ▶ Crusades. Between 1150 and 1250 the castle was built and made bigger, housing up to 2,000 soldiers at one time. The castle has an outside wall with thirteen towers and an inside wall, which is higher than the outside wall so that the defenders of the castle always had an advantage over their attackers. Between the two walls is a moat, which provided water for the horses and taking baths. In the middle of the castle is a courtyard. Another interesting aspect of the castle is the big stone hill on the south side of the castle, which is very hard to climb and gave extra protection against attackers. In 1271, the castle went under attack. The 200 knights who defended it lost and gave up their castle to a Muslim army. *p. 35*

Old City of Jerusalem and its Walls (proposed [*vorgeschlagen für*] the World Heritage list): Jerusalem is a city in Israel and one of the oldest cities in the world. Although it is not listed as a World Heritage Site, it has a lot of history to offer. It is a holy city for Jewish, Christian and Muslim people. There are over 220 important monuments in Jerusalem, but the most significant is the Dome of the Rock, which was built and finished during the 7th century. The Dome of the Rock is the place where Christians, Jews and Muslims believe Abraham almost killed his son for God, until God sent him a lamb instead. Another important site in Jerusalem is the Wailing Wall (*Klagemauer*), also known as the Western Wall. The wall is believed to be a part of the ruins from a very old, important temple and it is the holiest place for the Jewish people. Many people go there every year to pray, or they send prayers on pieces of paper, which are rolled up and put into small holes in the wall. *p. 33*

Palace and Park of Versailles: During the late 1600s, King Louis XIII began building a hunting lodge (*Jagdschloss*). Later, his son ▶ Louis XIV began to work on the building: he hired architects to make it much bigger, and after some time, they turned it into a beautiful palace. Louis XIV did not only expand the building, but also the gardens. He made sure that they were just as impressive as the palace. It took over forty years to design and to finish the garden. From 1682 to 1790, the Palace of Versailles was the official French palace and three different kings lived there. Each of them made their own changes and added to it. Other kings and queens in Europe used the palace as a model to design their own royal homes. One interesting thing to see when visiting the palace is the Queen's Hamlet (*Weiler oder kleines Dorf der Königin*). Marie Antoinette (Queen of France, who was married to Louis XVI) built this little village behind the palace, where she lived for a few months each year. Everyone, even the King, had to ask for permission to visit the village. There are twelve buildings and during Marie Antoinette's lifetime, it was a farm with workers who lived there. *p. 74*

Palestine: Palestine is a region located on the eastern coast of the Mediterranean Sea. It is a very important area to Jews, Christians and Muslims because many important events took place there. Jewish people believe that God promised them the land. Christians think the land is important because Jesus lived there, and Muslims think it is important because their prophet Muhammad went up to heaven in Palestine. One famous historical site in Palestine is the Church of the Nativity in Bethlehem, which was built over the area where it is believed that Jesus was born. It is one of the oldest Christian churches in the world and was built in 229 AD. Each year, many Christian pilgrims take a journey to the church and stop at other important religious sites, like the field where the angels told the shepherds about Jesus' birth. *p. 30*

Potosí: Potosí is located in southern Bolivia and is one of the highest cities in the world at 4,050 meters. The mountain overlooking the town, Cerro Rico ("Rich Mountain"), has thousands of mines inside of it. In 1545, silver was discovered in the mountain and many people moved there to become rich. After just thirty years, more than 150,000 people lived in Potosí, making it the city with the most people in the ▶ 'New World' at that time. Due to a decrease in silver production and a typhus epidemic which killed 22,000 people who lived there, only 20,000 people lived in the city by the early 1800s. Today Potosí is still an important mining city: silver, tin (*Zinn*), copper (*Kupfer*) and other metals can be found here. It also has many interesting sights to visit, such as the Church of San Lorenzo, the houses where the silver miners lived, some historical houses where very wealthy people lived, and an interesting water system. *p. 56*

Seville Cathedral: Seville Cathedral is also known as the Cathedral of Saint Mary of the See. It is a Roman Catholic cathedral, located in Seville, Andalusia, Spain. It is the largest church in Spain and the third largest church in Europe. It contains over 80 chapels. In the 12th century, a mosque stood where the cathedral is today. The mosque was changed into a church in 1248 when Ferdinand III of Castile conquered the city. Several parts of the mosque still exist today, such as the Abluciones courtyard and the Puerta del Perdón door. One interesting site to see at the church is the grave of ▶ Christopher Colombus. *p. 56*

St. Michael's Church at Hildesheim: This church, located about 30 km southeast of Hannover, was built between 1010 and 1020. It is a very important example of art from the ▶ Middle Ages. Especially interesting is the wooden ceiling (*Decke*), painted in 1230, which shows a Tree of Jesse (the family tree of Jesus). It is the only flat church ceiling found in Germany. The bronze doors and bronze column are also important parts of the church. They show scenes from the Book of Genesis (*Schöpfungsgeschichte*) and Christ's life. *p. 6*

Tenochtitlán: Tenochtitlán was a city built on an island in a shallow lake in Mexico, founded in 1325. Its ruins are located in the central part of modern day Mexico City. During the 15th century, Tenochtitlán became the capital of the ▶ Aztec Empire and had a population of 212,000 people. At that time, it was the biggest city in the world. The city was very modern and clean, with temples, art, medicine, busy marketplaces and aqueducts, which provided clean drinking water. In the marketplaces, people traded their goods with each other and did not use money. There was also the palace of Monteczuma II, which had a zoo with many different species of animals and a garden with many different kinds of plants. In 1521, the city was taken over by the Spanish. This was the beginning of the end of the Aztec civilization. The Spanish Conquistador ▶ Hernán Cortés ordered his men to destroy the Aztec city. A new city was built for the Spanish. *p. 54*

Wartburg Castle: Wartburg is a castle, located on top of a 410 meter cliff in Eisenach, Germany. The construction of the castle began in 1067 by Count Ludwig der Springer. There are two courtyards, a palace with three floors, several wooden buildings and a water tank on the property. The palace's walls look the same as they did during the ▶ Middle Ages, except for the tapestries, paintings and mosaics which were added in 1900. The castle is most famous because ▶ Martin Luther translated the Bible into German while he was hiding at the castle from 1521 to 1522. Martin Luther's study can still be seen by visitors today; it looks just as it did while Martin Luther was living there. *p. 60*

English-German vocabulary

A

abbey *Kloster*
abbot *Abt*
ability *Fähigkeit*
(to) abolish sth. *etw. abschaffen*
(to) accept sth. *etw. hinnehmen, akzeptieren*
acorn *Eichel*
account *hier: Bericht*
accurate **['ækjərət]** *genau, exakt, akkurat*
(to) act as proof *als Beweis dienen*
actually *tatsächlich*
AD (= anno Domini) *nach Christi Geburt*
(in) addition (to) zusätzlich
(to) admit sth. *etw. zugeben*
advantage *Vorteil*
advice (sg., no pl.) *Rat, Ratschläge*
afterwards *hinterher*
age *hier: Zeitalter / (Zeit)Alter*
Age of Discovery *Zeitalter der Entdeckungen*
Age of Reformation *Zeitalter der Reformation*
(to) agree *zustimmen*
aim (noun) *Ziel, Absicht*
alliance **[ə'laɪəns]** *Bündnis, Allianz*
(to) allow sth. *etw. erlauben*
although *obwohl*
a.m. = ante meridiem/before midday *vormittags*
amazed *überrascht, verblüfft*
ambassador *Botschafter/in*
amount of *Menge an*
(to) analyse sth. *etw. analysieren*
ancient **['eɪnʃənt]** *alt, altertümlich, antik, klassisch*
ankle *Knöchel*
annunciation *Verkündigung*
(to) appear *erscheinen, auftauchen*
(to) apply for sth. *sich um etw. bewerben*
(to) appoint sb. *jdn. ernennen*
apprentice *Lehrling*
aqueduct **['ækwɪdʌkt]** *Aquäduct, Wasserleitung*
Arab *Araber/in*
Arabic *arabisch*
(arch-)bishop **[ɑ:tʃ-]** *(Erz-)Bischof*
(to) argue *streiten, argumentieren*
armour *Rüstung*
arms *hier: Wappen*
army *Armee, Heer*
arrival *Ankunft*
(to) arrest sb. *jdn. verhaften*
arrow *Pfeil*
arsenal *Arsenal, Waffenlager*
art *Kunst*
artist *Künstler/in*
as *hier: während*
as a consequence *daher, folglich, demzufolge*
as a result *daher, folglich*
Asia Minor *Kleinasien*
aside (adv.) *beiseite*
astonishing *erstaunlich*
(to) attack sb./sth. *jdn./etw. angreifen, attackieren*
attack (noun) *Angriff*
attacker *Angreifer/in*
attractive *reizvoll, anziehend*
audience *Publikum, Zuhörer, Zuschauer, Leserschaft*

B

backward *rückständig*
bailey *Burghof*
ban (noun) *(offizielles) Verbot*
(to) ban sth. *etw. (offiziell) verbieten*
bankrupt *bankrott, pleite*
banner *Fahne*
barber *Friseur, Barbier*
battle (noun) *Schlacht*
BC (=before Christ) *vor Christi Geburt*
(to) be allowed to hunt *das Jagdrecht besitzen*
(to) beat sb./sth. *jdn./etw. schlagen*
(to) become used to sth. *sich an etw. gewöhnen*
beggar *Bettler/in*
behaviour *Verhalten*
(to) be indebted *verschuldet sein*
Belgium *Belgien*
belief *Glaube(n), Überzeugung*
bench *Bank*
(to) benefit from sth. *von etw. profitieren*
(to) be responsible for sth. *für etw. verantwortlich sein*
(to) be situated *gelegen sein*
(to) be surrounded by sth. *von etw. umgeben sein*
Bible *Bibel*
birth *Geburt*
bishop *Bischof*
blacksmith *Schmied/in*
(to) bless sb. *jdn. segnen*
(to) boil sth. *etw. kochen*
book illumination *Buchmalerei*
border *Grenze*
(to) borrow sth. *etw. ausleihen, hier: entlehnen*
both *beide*
bows and arrows *Pfeil und Bogen*
(at the) bottom *hier: am unteren Ende*
bright *hell, leuchtend*
bucket *Eimer*
bump *Beule*
butcher *Schlachter, Metzger*
Byzantine **[baɪ'zæntaɪn]** *byzantinisch*

C

Calicut *Kalkutta, heute: Kozhikode in Südindien*
(to) call for sth. *nach etw. rufen*
Canary Islands *Kanarische Inseln*
candelabra *Kandelaber, Armleuchter*
candle *Kerze*
candlestick *Kerzenhalter*
Cape of Good Hope *Kap der Guten Hoffnung*
capital *hier: Hauptstadt*
caption *Bildtext, Beschriftung, Bildlegende*
cargo *Ladung*
carpet *Teppich*
carriage *Kutsche*
cart *Karren*
cartoon *Karikatur, Spottbild*
cartoonist *Karikaturist/in*
castle *Burg, Schloss*
cat *"Katze", überdachtes Belagerungsgerät*
cattle *Vieh, Rinder*
(to) cause sth. *etw. verursachen*
cause (noun) *Ursache*
century *Jahrhundert*
chaincoat *Kettenhemd*
chapel *Kapelle*
characteristic *Kennzeichen, Eigenschaft*
(to) check sth. *etw. überprüfen*
(to) check on sth. *etw. kontrollieren*
cheerfulness *Fröhlichkeit*
chest *hier: Truhe*
(to) chew sth. *etw. kauen*
chief *Häuptling*
Christ *Jesus Christus*
Christian *christlich, Christ*
Christianity *Christentum*
church *Kirche, Kirchengebäude*
(the) Church *die Kirche (als Institution)*
(the) Church of the Holy Sepulchre *Grabeskirche*
churches *hier: Konfessionen (religiöse Gruppen innerhalb einer Religion)*
churchman *Geistlicher*
citizen *Bürger/in, Stadtbewohner/in*
city council *Stadtrat*
city state *Stadtstaat*
civil war *Bürgerkrieg*
(to) claim sth. *etw. verlangen*
clergy *Geistlichkeit, Klerus*
cloth *Tuch*
codex *Kodex, alte Buchform*
column **['kɒləm ★ 'kɑ:ləm]** *Säule*
common people *einfache Leute*
company *Firma, Unternehmen*
(to) compete with sb./sth. *mit jdn./etw. konkurrieren*
(to) complain about sth. *sich über etw. beschweren, beklagen*
composer *Komponist/in*
(to) confront *konfrontieren*
(to) conquer sth. *etw. erobern*
consequence *Folge, Auswirkung, Konsequenz*
consequently *foglich*
(to) contain sth. *etw. enthalten*
content (adj.) *zufrieden*
content (noun) *Inhalt*
(to) contrast sth. *etw. kontrastieren, gegenüberstellen*

convent *Konvent, Kloster*
(to) convince sb. *jdn. überzeugen*
costume *Kostüm*
corn *Mais*
(to) cost, cost, cost *kosten*
cotton *Baumwolle*
council *Rat*
(to) count (noun) *zählen*
count *hier: Graf*
counter argument *Gegenargument*
court *Hof, Hofstaat*
cover *Titelseite*
craft *Handwerk*
craftsman *Handwerker*
(to) create sth. *etw. (er)schaffen, erstellen*
crew *Mannschaft, Besatzung*
crime *Verbrechen*
criticism *Kritik*
(to) criticize sb./sth. *jdn./etw. kritisieren*
crop *Ernte*
cross *Kreuz*
crossbowman *Bogenschütze*
crossroad *Kreuzung*
crowded *überfüllt*
cruel *grausam*
crusade **[kruːˈseɪd]** *Kreuzzug*
crusader *Kreuzfahrer/in*
(to) crush sb. *jdn. vernichten*
curiosity **[ˌkjʊəriˈɒsəti]** *Neugier, Wissbegier*
curtain *Vorhang*
customs duties **[djuːtiːz ★ duːtiːz]** *Zollabgaben/-gebühren*
(to) cut down *fällen, abholzen*

D

damnable *verdammenswert*
(to) dare sth. *etw. wagen*
debate (noun) *Debatte*
debts **[dets]** *Schulden*
to decide *(sich) entscheiden*
decree *Dekret, Urteil, Erlass*
(to) declare sth. *etw. erklären, verkünden*
(to) defeat *besiegen*
defeat (noun) *Niederlage*
(to) defend sb./sth. *jmdn./etw. verteidigen*
defender *Verteidiger/in*
(to) degenerate **[dɪˈdʒenəreɪt]** *herunterkommen, sich zurückentwickeln*
demand (noun) *Forderung*
(to) demand sth. *etw. verlangen, fordern*
demon *Dämon*
depth *Tiefe*
(to) destroy sth. *etw. zerstören*
detailed *detailliert, genau*
(to) develop sth. *etw. entwickeln*
devil *Teufel*
diagram *schematische Darstellung, Diagramm*
diameter *Durchmesser*
dice (pl.) *Würfel*
Diet *hier: Reichstag*
(to) dig, dug, dug *graben*
(to) disagree (with sb./sth.) *(mit jdm./etw.) nicht einverstanden sein*
disappointed *enttäuscht*
(to) discover sth. *etw. entdecken*
discovery *Entdeckung*
disease *Krankheit*
dish *Gericht, Speise*
dishonest **[dɪsˈɒnɪst]** *unehrlich*
(to) dismiss sb. *jdn. entlassen*
(to) dissect sth. *etw. sezieren*
dissection *das Sezieren*
distrust (noun) *Misstrauen*
divine **[dɪˈvaɪn]** right *Gottesgnadentum*
(to) dominate *vorherrschen, dominieren*
donkey *Esel*
dormitory *Schlafsaal*
drawbridge *Zugbrücke*
(to) drive (drove, driven) off *vertreiben*
dues *Abgaben (in Form von Geld, Waren oder Dienstleistungen)*
Duke *Herzog*
Dutch (noun/adj.) *Holländer (pl.), holländisch*
duty *Pflicht*
dye *hier: Stofffarbe*

E

(to) be eager for sth. *begierig auf etw. sein*
(to) earn a living *seinen Lebensunterhalt verdienen*
(to) educate sb. **[ˈedʒukeɪt]** *jdn. erziehen, ausbilden*
effect *Auswirkung, Effekt*
(to) elect sb. *jdn. wählen*
emblem *Wappen, Abzeichen*
(to) embroider *besticken*
(to) emigrate *auswandern*
emperor *Kaiser, Herrscher*
Empire *(Kaiser-)Reich, Imperium*
(to) emphasize sth. *etw. betonen*
(to) encourage *(sb. to do sth.)* **[ɪnˈkʌrɪdʒ]** *(jdn.) ermutigen (etw. zu tun)*
enemy *Feind/in*
engine *Maschine*
engineer *Ingenieur/in, Bauleiter/in*
enlightenment *Aufklärung*
epidemic (noun) *Seuche, Epidemie*
equal *gleich*
(to) establish sth. *etw. einrichten, gründen, bilden, errichten*
estate *(gesellschaftlicher) Stand*
(to) estimate sth. *etw. schätzen*
event *Ereignis*
evidence (sg.) *Beweis(e)*
(to) exaggerate sth. **[ɪgˈzædʒəreɪt]** *etw. übertreiben*
(to) excavate sth. *etw. ausgraben*
except *außer*
exchange (noun/verb) *Austausch/austauschen*
(to) excommunicate *exkommunizieren, aus der Kirche ausschließen*
(to) execute sb. *jdn. hinrichten*
(to) expand sth. *etw. vergrößern, ausbreiten*
(to) expect *erwarten*
experience *Erfahrung, Erlebnis*
experiment *Experiment*
(to) explore sth. *etw. erforschen*
(to) export sth. *etw. ausführen, exportieren*
export (noun) *Ausfuhr, Export*
extract (from) *Auszug (aus)*

F

fabric *Stoff, Tuch*
failure **[ˈfeɪljə(r)]** *Misserfolg, Versagen*
faith *Glaube*
(to) fascinate *faszinieren*
fashionable *modisch, schick*
(to) favour sb./sth. *jdn./etw. bevorzugen*
favour (noun) *Gefälligkeit, Gunst*
feast day *Feiertag*
(to) fear sth. *etw. (be)fürchten*
fee *Gebühr*
(to) fight, fought, fought *(be)kämpfen*
fine (noun) *Strafgebühr*
finished goods *Fertigwaren*
(to) fire *(ab)feuern*
fireplace *Kamin*
flat *flach*
(to) flatter sb. *jdn. schmeicheln*
(to) flee, fled, fled *flüchten, fliehen*
flood (noun) *Flut, Überflutung*
(to) flow *fließen*
flower bed *Blumenbeet*
follower *Anhänger/in, Jünger/in*
foot soldier *Fußsoldat*
(to) force sb. *jdn. zwingen*
forest *Wald*
forever *für immer, ewig*
(to) forbid, forbade, forbidden sth. *etw. verbieten*
(to) forgive, forgave, forgiven sb. *jdn. vergeben, jdm. verzeihen*
forgiveness *Verzeihung, Vergebung*
(to) form an alliance *ein Bündnis schließen*
former *frühere, früherer, früheres*
fortress *Festung*
fortune *Vermögen*
(to) found sth. *etw. gründen*
fountain *Springbrunnen*
(to) free sb. *jdn. befreien*
freedom *Freiheit*
French *französisch*
from afar *von ferne*
funeral *Bestattung*
fur coat **[fɜː(r)]** *Pelzmantel*

G

(to) gamble *(Glücksspiele) spielen, um Geld*

spielen
gate *Stadttor*
gatehouse *Wachturm*
ghetto *Ghetto; Stadtviertel, in dem überwiegend eine bestimmte gesellschaftliche, häufig sozial ausgegrenzte Gruppe lebt*
(to) give advice to sb. *jdn. beraten*
glass beads *Glasperlen*
glow (noun) *Leuchten*
goods *Waren, Güter*
(to) govern *regieren*
government *Regierung*
governor *hier: Statthalter/in, Gouverneur/in*
grain *Korn*
grapes *Weintrauben*
gravedigger *Totengräber/in*
Greek, Greece *griechisch, Griechenland*
growth *Wachstum*
(to) guard *bewachen*
guild **[gɪld]** *Gilde*
gun *Gewehr*

H

hangman *Henker*
harvest *Ernte*
(to) have a say (in sth.) *bei etw. Mitspracherecht haben*
(to) have a say *etw. zu sagen haben, etw. bestimmen*
(to) have an effect on sth./sb. *eine Wirkung auf etw./jdn. haben*
head *Kopf, Oberhaupt*
(to) heat *heizen*
heathen (noun/adj.) **['hiːðn]** *Heide/Heidin, heidnisch*
heaven *(biblischer) Himmel*
heavenly *himmlisch*
hedge *Hecke, Gebüsch*
hell *Hölle*
hellish *höllisch*
helmet *Helm*
(to) herd cattle *Vieh hüten*
highest-ranking *hochrangigste/er/es*
high-heeled *hochhackig*
hint *Hinweis*
historian *Historiker/in*
holy *heilig*
Holy Communion *Heilige Kommunion*
Holy Roman Empire of German Nation *Heiliges Römisches Reich Deutscher Nation*
however *jedoch*
human (noun) **['hjuːmən]** *Mensch*
human (adj.) *menschlich*
human body *menschlicher Körper, Leiche*
humility **[ˌhjuː'mɪləti]** *Demut*
(to) hunt sth. *etw. jagen*

I

(to) identify *hier: bestimmen, ermitteln*
illness *Krankheit*
(to) imagine sth. *sich etw. vorstellen*
(to) import sth. *etw. importieren, einführen*
import (noun) *Einfuhr, Import*
important *wichtig*
(to) impose sth. *etw. auferlegen*
impressive *beeindruckend*
(to) include sth. *etw. einschließen, einfügen*
income *Einkommen*
in contrast to *im Gegensatz zu*
(to) increase sth. *etw. erhöhen*
increase (noun) *Erhöhung*
independent *unabhängig*
indebted **[ɪn'detɪd]** *verschuldet*
indulgence **[ɪn'dʌldʒəns]** *Ablass*
inhabitant *Einwohner/in*
(to) inherit sth. *etw. erben*
ink *Tinte*
inland *Inland*
inn *Gasthaus*
innkeeper *Gastwirt/in*
instead *stattdessen*
instead of *anstatt von*
intention *Absicht*
(to) invent sth. *etw. erfinden*
invention *Erfindung*
inventor *Erfinder*
iron *Eisen*
ivory *Elfenbein*

J

Jew *Jude/Jüdin*
Jewish people *jüdische Bevölkerung*
journey *Reise*
journeyman *reisender Handwerksgeselle*
jousting scene *Turnierszene*
(to) judge sth./sb. *jdn./etw. beurteilen*
judge (noun) *Richter/in*
juggler *Jongleur*
just as *genau wie*
justice *Gerechtigkeit*
(to) justify sth. *etw. rechtfertigen*

K

(to) keep close watch on sb./sth. *jdn./etw. scharf beobachten*
key *hier: (Karten-)Legende, Bilderklärung*
key term *Schlüsselbegriff*
(a) kind of *eine Art von*
king *König*
King's Council *Ratgeber des Königs, Kabinett*
knacker **['nækə(r)]** *Abdecker/in*
knight **[naɪt]** *Ritter*
knowledge **['nɒlɪdʒ]** *Wissen*

L

(to) label sth. *etw. beschriften*
lace *Spitze (Borte)*
lance *Lanze*
landlord *Landbesitzer, Grundherr*
landowner *Landbesitzer/in*
landscape *Landschaft*
landscape gardener *Landschaftsgärtner/in*
(to) last *andauern*
Latin *Latein*
latrine *Latrine, einfache Toilette*
law *Gesetz*
layman *Laie*
laziness *Faulheit*
(to) lead, led, led *führen, leiten*
leader *Anführer/in*
learned *gebildet*
lens *Linse*
lice (pl.) *Läuse*
lifelike *naturgetreu*
(to) light, lit, lit sth. *etw. erleuchten*
(to) limit sth. *etw. beschränken, begrenzen*
living (noun) *hier: Lebensunterhalt*
livres *französische Währung im 17. Jh.*
loan wort *Lehnwort*
local *örtlich*
long-distance merchant *Fernhandelskaufmann*
long-term cause *Langzeitursache*
lord *Herr, Lord*
(to) loot sth. *etw. plündern, ausrauben*
loss *Verlust*
lowly *niedrig, gering*
Lutheran *Lutheraner/in*

M

magazine *Speicher, Warenlager*
mainland *Festland*
(to) make sure *sicherstellen*
(to) maltreat sb. *jdn. misshandeln*
manor *Rittergut*
manure **[mən'jʊə(r)]** *Dünger*
map maker *Kartenzeichner/in, Kartograph/in*
marquis **['mɑːkwɪs]** *Graf*
mass *Messe, Gottesdienst*
master *Handwerksmeister/in*
meadow **['medəʊ]** *Weide, Wiese*
meaning *Bedeutung*
means (sg./pl.) *Mittel*
measure (noun) *Maßnahme*
medieval **[ˌmedi'iːvl]** also **[ˌmiːd-]** *mittelalterlich*
Mediterranean See *Mittelmeer*
(to) melt *schmilzen, schmelzen*
member *Mitglied*
(to) mention *erwähnen, nennen*
merchant **['mɜːtʃənt]** *Kaufmann, Händler/in*
message *Botschaft, Mitteilung*

Middle Ages *Mittelalter*
mine *Bergwerk*
minority *Minderheit*
misery *Elend*
moat *Burggraben*
monarch **['mɒnək]** *Monarch/in*
monastery **[ˌmɒnəstri]** *Kloster*
moneylender *Geldverleiher/in*
monk *Mönch*
mosque **[mɒsk]** *Moschee*
mouth *hier: Mündung*
mule *Maultier*
Muslim *Muslim/in*

N

narrow *schmal*
native (noun, adj.) *Einheimische/r, einheimisch abwertend: Eingeborener*
navigation *Schifffahrt*
necessary *notwendig*
New World *die Neue Welt = Amerika*
nightmare *Albtraum*
nobility *Adel*
noble (adj./noun) *edel, adlig / Adlige/r*
(to) notice sth. *etw. bemerken*
novel *Roman*
nowadays *heutzutage*
number *Anzahl*
numeral *Zahlensymbol*
nun *Nonne*

O

(to) obey *gehorchen*
object *Objekt, Gegenstand*
observation *Beobachtung*
(to) observe sb./sth. *jdn./etw. beobachten*
office *Amt*
official (noun) *Amtsperson, Beamter/Beamtin*
official language *Amtssprache*
Old World *die Alte Welt = Europa, Asien und Afrika*
on average *im Durchschnitt*
onion *Zwiebel*
on pain of death *unter Androhung der Todesstrafe*
opinion *Meinung, Überzeugung*
(to) oppose sb./sth. *sich jdm./etw. entgegensetzen*
opposite (noun) *Gegenteil*
(to) order sth. *etw. befehlen*
order (noun) *Befehl, Anweisung*
outfit *Bekleidung*
outlaw *Ausgestoßene/r, Geächtete/r, Gesetzlose/r*
(to) overcome differences *hier: Meinungsverschiedenheiten überwinden*
(to) oversee sth. *etw. überwachen*
(to) own sth. *etw. besitzen*
owner *Besitzer/in*

P

pamphlet *Broschüre, Flugblatt, Pamphlet*
past (noun) *Vergangenheit*
pasture **[pɑːstʃə(r)]** *Weideland*
(to) patrol *patroullieren*
patron **['peɪtrən]** *Förderer, Kunstmäzen*
(to) pave *pflastern, befestigen*
pay (noun) *Bezahlung, Lohn*
peace *Frieden*
peace talks *Friedensgespräche*
peach *Pfirsich*
pear *Birne*
peasant **['peznt]** *(mittelalterliche/r) Bauer/Bäuerin*
Peasants' Rebellion *Bauernaufstände*
Peasants' War *Bauernkrieg*
peddler *Hausierer/in*
per cent *Prozent*
period *(Zeit-)Abschnitt*
(to) persecute sb. **[ˌpɜːsɪkjuːt]** *jdn. verfolgen*
(to) persuade sb. **[pə'sweid]** *jdn. überzeugen*
pilgrim *Pilger/in*
pilgrimage *Pilgerreise, Pilgerschaft*
pineapple *Ananas*
play (noun) *hier: Drama, Theaterstück*
playwright *Dramatiker/in*
(to) plunder sth. *etw. plündern*
p.m. = post meridiem/after midday *nachmittags*
(to) point sth. out *auf etw. hinweisen*
pond *Teich*
pope *Papst*
population *Bevölkerung*
population loss *Bevölkerungsverlust*
porridge *Haferbrei*
port *Hafen*
possession *Besitz*
post *hier: Amt*
(to) pour sth. **[pɔː(r)]** *etw. eingießen, gießen*
power *Macht, Gewalt*
powerful *mächtig*
(to) practice a religion *eine Religion ausüben*
(to) praise sb./sth. *jdn./etw. loben, lobpreisen*
(to) pray *beten*
prayer book *Gebetsbuch*
prediction *Vorhersage*
(to) prefer sb./sth. *jdn./etw. bevorzugen*
prejudice *Vorurteil*
(to) pretend *vorgeben, so tun als ob*
(to) prevent sth. *etw. verhindern*
previously *vorher*
priest *Priester, Pfarrer*
prime minister *Ministerpräsident/in, Premierminister/in*
prince *hier: Fürst*
principle *Prinzip*
print (noun) *Druck*
(to) print sth. *etw. drucken*
printing *Buchdruck*
printing press *Druckerpresse*
prisoner *Gefangene/r*
prisoner of war *Kriegsgefangene/r*
privilege **[ˌprɪvəlɪdʒ]** *Privileg, Sonderrechte*
(to) produce sth.vetw. anfertigen, produzieren
(to) promise sth. *etw. versprechen*
proof *Beweis*
(to) protect sb./sth. *jdn./etw. schützen*
protection *Schutz*
(to) prove sth. *etw. beweisen, belegen*
proud *stolz*
public (adj.) / publicly (adv.) *öffentlich*
(to) publish sth. *etw. veröffentlichen*
(to) punish sb. *jdn. bestrafen*
punishment *Bestrafung*
purgatory **['pɜːgətri]** *Fegefeuer*
purpose *Zweck*
pustule *Pustel, Eiterbläschen*
(to) put sb. on trial (for sth.) *jdn. (wegen etw.) vor Gericht stellen*
(to) put sth. aside *etw. beiseitelegen*

R

race *„Rasse", Geschlecht*
radical *kompromisslos, radikal*
(to) raise sth. *hier: etw. hochziehen; erhöhen, anheben*
Ramadan fast *Ramadan, islamischer Fastenmonat*
rank (noun) *Rang*
rapier *Degen*
rare *selten, rar*
raw material *Rohstoff*
(to) reach sth. *etw. erreichen*
reason *Grund*
(to) rebel (against sth./sb.) *rebellieren, sich (gegen etw./jdn) auflehnen*
rebirth *Wiedergeburt*
recipient *Empfänger/in*
(to) recognize sb./sth. *jmd./etw. (wieder-/an-) erkennen*
redrawing *Nachzeichnung*
(to) reduce sth. *etw. vermindern, reduzieren*
(to) re-establish sth. *etw. neu einrichten*
reeve *Vogt, Verwalter*
(to) refuse sth. *etw. ablehnen*
reformation *Reformation, Erneuerung*
(to) regard sb./sth. *jdn./etw. betrachten*
relationship *Beziehung*
relative *Verwandte/r*
(to) remove sth. *etw. entfernen*
rent (noun) *Miete*
representative (noun) *Vertreter/in, Repräsent-*

ant/in, Abgeordnete/r
resistance *Widerstand*
responsible *verantwortlich*
result (noun) *Folge, Resultat*
revenge *Rache*
revolution *Revolution, Umsturz*
reward (noun) *Belohnung*
Rhineland-Palatinate *Reinland-Pfalz*
rice *Reis*
(to) rise, rose, risen *aufgehen, (auf)steigen, sich erheben*
rival (noun) *Rivale/Rivalin, Konkurrent/in*
(to) rob sb. *jdn. (aus)rauben, (be)rauben*
rock (noun) *Felsen*
Roman, Rome *römisch, Rom*
roof *Dach*
route *Weg, Route*
routine **[ruː'tiːn]** *Routine, Tagesablauf*
royal *königlich*
rumour *Gerücht*
rumour has it that ... *Gerüchte besagen, dass ...*
rule (noun) *Regel, Herrschaft*
(to) rule *herrschen, regieren*
ruler *hier: Herrscher/in, Machthaber/in*
(to) run sth. *etw. (eine Firma, eine Schule) führen, regieren*

S

(to) sacrifice sb./sth. *jdn./etw. opfern*
safe *sicher*
safety *Sicherheit*
(to) sail *segeln*
saint *Heilige/r*
(to) save sb./sth. *jdn./etw. retten, erlösen*
scaling ladder *Sturmleiter*
sceptre **[septə(r)]** *Zepter*
scholar **['skɒlə(r)]** *Gelehrte/r*
science **['saɪəns]** *Wissenschaft*
scientific *wissenschaftlich*
(to) seal an order *die Gültigkeit eines Befehls besiegeln*
(in)addition (to). *zusätzlich*
(to) search sb./sth. *jdn./etw. durchsuchen*
secretly (adv.) *heimlich, insgeheim*
series *Serie, Abfolge*
sermon *Predigt*
servant *Diener/in*
settler *Siedler/in*
shadow *Schatten*
shallow *flach*
(to) share sth. *etw. teilen*
(to) shave *(sich) rasieren*
shield (noun) *Waffen-/Schutzschild*
shiny *glänzend*
(to) shoot, shot, shot *schießen*
shopkeeper *Ladeninhaber/in*
shrine *Heiligenschrein*
shutter *Fensterladen*
siege **[siːdʒ]** *Belagerung*
(to) sign sth. **[saɪn]** *etw. unterzeichnen*
silk *Seide*
sin *Sünde*
sinful *sündhaft*
(to be) situated **['sɪtʃueɪtɪd]** *gelegen (sein), sich befinden*
(to) slaughter **['slɔːtə(r)]** *schlachten*
slave *Sklave/Sklavin*
slit *Schlitz*
smallpox *Pocken*
so-called *sogenannt*
society **[sə'saɪəti]** *Gesellschaft*
solar system *Sonnensystem*
soldier **['səʊldʒe(r)]** *Soldat/in*
soul *Seele*
source *Quelle*
spark *Zündfunke*
spear *Spieß*
sphere **[sfɪə(r)]** *hier: Erdkugel*
spice *Gewürz*
(to) spin, spun, spun *hier: spinnen (auch: sich drehen)*
splendid *prächtig*
(to) spread, spread, spread **[spred]** *sich ausbreiten, verbreiten*
(to) stab sb. *jdn. niederstechen*
(to) stand for sth. *für etw. stehen, etw. bedeuten*
(to) starve *verhungern*
state income *Staatseinkommen*
stately *herrschaftlich*
stocking *Strumpf*
stool *Schemel*
stomach *Bauch*
(to) store sth. *etw. aufbewahren*
(to) strangle sb. *jdn. erwürgen*
straw *Stroh*
stream *Strom, Bach*
subject (noun) *hier: Untertan/in*
success **[sək'ses]** *Erfolg*
successful *erfolgreich*
sudden *plötzlich*
(to) suffer from sth. *unter etw. leiden*
suffering *Leid, Leiden (noun)*
(to) be superior to sth./sb. *besser als etw./jd. sein*
(to) support sb./sth. *jdn./etw. unterstützen*
(to) be surrounded by sth. **[sə'raʊndɪd]** *von etw. umgeben von*
(to) swear, swore, sworn *schwören, fluchen*
sword **[sɔːd]** *Schwert*
system of sewers *Kanalsystem, Kanalisation*

T

(to) take measures **[meʒə(r)]** *Maßnahmen ergreifen*
(to) take part in sth. *an etw. teilnehmen*
(to) take possession of sb./sth. *jdn./etw. in Besitz nehmen*
(to) take prisoner *gefangen nehmen*
(to) take revenge (on sb.) *Rache üben, sich (an jdm.) rächen*
tapestry *Wandteppich*
tax *Steuer, Abgabe*
(to) teach sb. *jdn. unterrichten, lehren*
teaching *Lehre*
tension *Spannung*
terms *Bestimmungen (in einem Vertrag)*
theology *Theologie*
theory *Theorie*
thesis **[θiːsis]**, *pl. theses* **['θiːsiːz]** *These, Thesen*
throughout (the Middle Ages) *während des ganzen/gesamten (Mittelalters)*
throughout Europe *in ganz Europa*
thus *deswegen, folglich*
tiled *gekachelt, gefliest*
tithe **[taɪð]** *der (Kirchen-)Zehnte, Kirchensteuer*
tobacco *Tabak*
toll *Zoll, Mautgebühren*
tonsure **['tɒnʃə(r)]** *Tonsur, geschorene Haartracht bei Mönchen*
towards *in Richtung, entgegen*
track *Feldweg*
(to) trade *(mit etw.) handeln*
trade (noun) *Handel*
trade route *Handelsweg*
trading company *Handelsgesellschaft*
(to) translate sth. *etw. übersetzen*
treasure **['treʒə(r)]** *Schatz*
(to) treat sb. *jdn. (schlecht, gut) behandeln*
trebuchet *Blide, Wurfschleuder*
trial *Gerichtsverfahren*
triangular *dreieckig*
triangular trade across the Atlantic *Transatlantischer Dreieckshandel*
troops *Truppen*
truth *Wahrheit*
Turk *Türke/Türkin*
turkey *Truthahn*
turmoil *Aufruhr*
tusk *Stoßzahn*
typhus *Typhus, Fleckfieber*

U

umbilical cord *Nabelschnur*
uncivilized **[ʌnˌsɪvəlaɪzd]** *unzivilisiert*
uncomfortable **[ʌnˌkʌmftəbl]** *unbequem, ungemütlich*
unfair *ungerecht*
unity **['juːnəti]** *Einheit*
universe **['juːnɪvɜːs]** *Universum*
unlimited *grenzenlos, unbegrenzt*
(to) use force *Gewalt anwenden*

V

veil *Schleier*
velvet *Samt*
victim *Opfer*
victory *Sieg*
view [vjuː] *hier: Sicht, Ausblick*
village *Dorf*
villager *Dorfbewohner/in*
villein *Leibeigene/r*
violent *gewaltsam, gewalttätig*
volunteer [ˌvɒlən'tɪə(r)] *Freiwillige/r*
voyage [vɔɪɪdʒ] *lange (See-)Reise*

W

war *Krieg*
warrior *Krieger/in*
waste *Abfall, hier: Abwasser*
waste water *Abwasser*
watch (noun) *hier: Wache*
wealth *Wohlstand, Reichtum*
wealthy *reich, wohlhabend*
weapon *Waffe*
(to) weave sth. *etw. weben*
well (noun) *Quelle, Pumpe*
well-fitting *passend, angemessen*
well-shaped *wohlgeformt*
wheat *Weizen*
wig *Perücke*
womb [wuːm] *Mutterleib, Gebärmutter*
woodcut *Holzschnitt*
workshop *Werkstatt*
World Heritage Site *Weltkulturerbe*
wound [wuːnd] *Wunde*

Y

yet *dennoch*

Words to learn

Unit 1
Life in the Middle Ages

1.2 Germany in the Middle Ages

AD (= anno Domini) *nach Christi Geburt*
age *hier: Zeitalter*
BC (= before Christ) *vor Christus*
Christ *Jesus Christus*
forest *Wald*
historian *Historiker*
inhabitant *Einwohner/in*
key term *Schlüsselbegriff*
medieval *mittelalterlich*
Middle Ages *Mittelalter*
on average *im Durchschnitt*
per cent *Prozent*
period *(Zeit-)Abschnitt*
village *Dorf*

1.3 The nobles and their castles

(to) be responsible *for sth. für etw. verantwortlich sein*
bench *Bank*
candle *Kerze*
castle *Burg, Schloss*
(to) heat *heizen*
important *wichtig*
mass *Messe, Gottesdienst*
noble (noun, adj.) *Adlige/r, adlig*
priest *Priester, Pfarrer*
servant *Diener/in*
waste *Abfall, Abwasser*
well *Brunnen*

1.4 From wooden castles to stone castles

(to) attack *angreifen*
bright *hell, leuchtend*
castle *Burg*
century *Jahrhundert*
churchman *Kirchenmann*
(to) decide *(sich) entscheiden*
(to) dig, dug, dug *graben*
emperor *Kaiser, Herrscher*
extract (from) *Auszug (aus)*
(to) fight, fought, fought *kämpfen*
(to) fire *(ab)feuern*
(to) forbid, forbade, forbidden *verbieten*
helmet *Helm*
(to) hunt *jagen*
knight *Ritter*
lord *Herr*
nobility *Adel*
noble *adlig*
pay (noun) *Bezahlung*
peasant *(mittelalterliche/r) Bäuerin/Bauer*
shield *Waffen-/Schutzschild*
(to) shoot, shot, shot *schießen*
soldier *Soldat*
sword *Schwert*
wealthy *reich, wohlhabend*
weapon *Waffe*

1.5 Life in a medieval village

duty *Pflicht, Aufgabe*
(to) guard *bewachen*
harvest *Ernte*
judge *Richter*
(to) loot *plündern*
(to) own *besitzen*
pilgrimage *Pilgerreise*
(to) pray *beten*
(to) produce *anfertigen, produzieren*
(to) rule *herrschen*
(to) share *teilen*
(to) support *unterstützen*
village *Dorf*

History skills: Analysing historical objects

(to) analyse sth. *etw. analysieren*
(to) create *erschaffen*
goods *Waren, Güter*
object *Objekt, Gegenstand*
owner *Besitzer/in*
past *Vergangenheit*
(to) prove *beweisen, belegen*
source *Quelle*
(to) trade *(mit etw.) handeln*

1.6 Life in a medieval monastery

(to) accept sth. *etw. hinnehmen, akzeptieren*
although *obwohl*
a.m. *vormittags*
(to) argue *streiten, argumentieren*
(to) check on sth. *etw. kontrollieren*
content (adj.) *zufrieden*
dormitory *Schlafsaal*
(to) educate *erziehen, ausbilden*
heaven *(biblischer) Himmel*
(to) inherit *erben*
(to) lead, led, led *führen*
monk *Mönch*
nun *Nonne*
outfit *Bekleidung*
p.m. *nachmittags*
(to) praise *loben, lobpreisen*
(to) punish *bestrafen*
reward (noun) *Belohnung*
routine *Routine, Tagesablauf*
(to) run the country *das Land regieren*

1.7 Everybody had to lead a good Christian life

(to) boil *kochen*
(to) chew *kauen*
devil *Teufel*
forever *für immer, ewig*
(to) forgive, forgave, forgiven *vergeben*
head *Kopf*
hell *Hölle*
(to) melt *schmilzen, schmelzen*
(to) pour *gießen*
reason *Grund*
soul *Seele*
(to) suffer *leiden*
tax *Steuer*

1.8 Life in a medieval town

advantage *Vorteil*
(to) agree *zustimmen*
(to) allow sth. *etw. erlauben*
attractive *reizvoll, anziehend*
birth *Geburt*
citizen *Bürger/in*
(to) complain *sich beklagen, sich beschweren*
content (noun) *Inhalt*
council *Rat*
(to) count *zählen*
craft *Handwerk*
craftsman *Handwerker*
crossroad *Kreuzung*
(to) defend *verteidigen*
(to) demand *verlangen, fordern*
dishonest *unehrlich*
(to) elect *wählen*
except *außer*
fine (noun) *Strafgebühr*
freedom *Freiheit*
funeral *Bestattung*
gate *(Stadt-)Tor*
goods *Waren, Güter*
government *Regierung*
(to) have a say *etw. zu sagen haben, etw. bestimmen*
illness *Krankheit*
income *Einkommen*
member *Mitglied*
merchant *Kaufmann*
narrow *eng*
(to) promise *versprechen*
protection *Schutz*
public *öffentlich*
purpose *Zweck*
(to) raise *hochziehen*
rank *Rang, Stellung*